Listen
Like You
Mean It

Listen Like You Mean It

Reclaiming the Lost Art
of True Connection

XIMENA VENGOECHEA

Portfolio / Penguin

Portfolio / Penguin
An imprint of Penguin Random House LLC
penguinrandomhouse.com

Most Portfolio books are available at a discount when purchased in quantity for sales promotions or corporate use. Special editions, which include personalized covers, excerpts, and corporate imprints, can be created when purchased in large quantities. For more information, please call (212) 572-2232 or e-mail specialmarkets@penguinrandomhouse.com. Your local bookstore can also assist with discounted bulk purchases using the Penguin Random House corporate Business-to-Business program. For assistance in locating a participating retailer, e-mail B2B@penguinrandomhouse.com.

Illustrations by the author.

Library of Congress Cataloging-in-Publication Data
Names: Vengoechea, Ximena, author.
Title: Listen like you mean it : reclaiming the lost art of true connection
/ Ximena Vengoechea.
Description: First Edition. | New York : Portfolio, 2021 | Includes index.
Identifiers: LCCN 2020039919 (print) | LCCN 2020039920 (ebook) |
ISBN 9780593087053 (hardcover) | ISBN 9780593087060 (ebook)
Subjects: LCSH: Listening.
Classification: LCC BF323.L5 V45 2021 (print) |
LCC BF323.L5 (ebook) | DDC 153.6/8—dc23
LC record available at https://lccn.loc.gov/2020039919
LC ebook record available at https://lccn.loc.gov/2020039920

Printed in the United States of America
1 3 5 7 9 10 8 6 4 2

Book design by Daniel Lagin

Some names and identifying characteristics have been changed
to protect the privacy of the individuals involved.

To my parents,
who have always made me feel heard

CONTENTS

To Listen Is to Understand

Charlotte was quiet, and so was I. We were sitting in the research lab, in front of a one-way mirror through which my team was observing the session. We had reached a crucial point in our conversation about a difficult and often-taboo topic: personal finances.

It's often easier to talk about pictures than to talk about something so intimate, so for this study on budgeting, I had asked participants to collect images of their ideal financial future to help guide our discussions. Each participant had a different vision for themselves. Some brought in pictures of luxury cars and extravagant homes to represent a future with more money than they needed, while others, like Charlotte, shared images that showed they aimed for that middle-class dream of home ownership and organic groceries. Still others brought images that indicated they longed for the bare necessities, like getting out of debt and out of the canned food aisle.

From my conversation with Charlotte so far, I knew that she was tired. She had quit a job she loved after having a baby to raise her son full time. Now, she filled her days with childcare and household planning while her husband worked. With a single salary and a third mouth to feed, her family budget had to be measured carefully. Every week she compared deals across local grocery stores, shopped creatively to keep her budget in check, and meal planned according to what was on sale. Every grocery run was carefully documented for her husband, who regularly reviewed their spending in an effort to keep their budget on track.

Some people enjoy the conquest of finding the best deals and will share these stories with pride and a glow in their eyes, but not Charlotte. She dutifully shared the necessary details with me, but I could tell she was not enjoying our conversation. She had increasingly begun to avoid eye contact, and her responses, once clear, were now little more than a mumble. My co-workers in the back room pinged me on Slack, "Can you ask her to speak up? Hard to hear back here."

When I asked Charlotte what she thought it would take to get to her ideal financial state—shopping for fancy cheese at gourmet markets instead of the sales at Safeway—she gave me what I knew was a surface-level answer, the kind you give to quickly placate someone without actually saying what you mean. Just like saying "fine" when someone asks you how you're doing, when you're actually having the worst day ever.

"More budgeting, I guess," she said. Then, she was silent, even a bit sullen. She sighed and looked away.

Sensing her unease, I wanted to let Charlotte off the hook and move on to the next topic. Part of me even wanted to bail her out entirely and say, "We're all done here. Have a great day!" I wanted to interrupt wherever her train of thought was going—because it looked like it was a very stressful place. But I knew that if I did, I'd lose my chance to hear what she needed to say. So instead of moving on, I waited. Five seconds turned into ten seconds, and ten seconds turned into twenty. The silence felt interminable. I focused on my breathing, in and out, in and out, and waited some more. She turned to look at me, and I softly, quietly, held eye contact. And just when things began to feel really awkward, Charlotte spoke.

"I guess I don't know how we'll get there," she said. "We want to buy a home, but it's hard enough deal-hunting for groceries. Anything beyond that feels impossible—I'm not sure more budgeting can change that."

Charlotte stopped, but I sensed she had more to say, so I summarized aloud what I had heard.

"It sounds like a difficult balance, to manage both your near-term needs and future dreams," I said.

"You have no idea," she said, and she proceeded to open up about her fears and frustrations.

A Researcher's Tool Kit

For the past seven years, I have refined my listening skills as a user researcher, manager, and mentor at some of Silicon Valley's top tech companies. My job is to understand the people who use or could someday use the various products we build, from mobile apps and websites to in-home devices and on-the-go experiences. With every conversation, I am required to quickly connect with strangers—sometimes on topics they don't want to talk about, and often in front of an audience—and discover what makes them tick, what drives them nuts, and how and why our products play a role in their lives. It's a challenging task, but a good researcher makes it feel natural and easy.

I've been a user researcher for nearly a decade now, but no matter how many sessions I've run, every interview has a moment like Charlotte's: a participant is on the verge of sharing something important, until their emotions, temperament, focus, or even a desire to please get in the way, causing them to shut down and clam up. When this happens, every ounce of my body wants to pivot, interrupt, or save participants (and myself) from discomfort.

But I've got a job to do. In every study, I have to uncover a specific set of insights that will ensure that my team is building a product that's actually useful—not just one they assume has potential. I have to know what a participant really thinks, whether by shadowing someone catching a rideshare to learn about their experience with a mobile app (*Do they obsessively track their driver's progress, or do they tuck away their phone and wait it out—and why?*), asking a traveler how it feels when a vacation rental listing doesn't line up with reality to help better set expectations in the future (*How inaccurate is too inaccurate? What is considered to be misleading and what's a simple mistake?*), or even prompting a group of participants to critique our app, site, or real-world experience to understand how we can improve it (*We know the app could be better—do they think so, too? If so, where should we start?*).

So I've learned to get comfortable with discomfort. I've learned how to lean into it and show the other person that I am interested in what they have to say, and how to confirm my understanding of what I'm hearing in the moment. I've learned that to truly connect and understand my participant, I need to stay active in conversation—not by rushing things along or persuading others to come around to my point of view, but by listening thoughtfully to what's being said, what's left unsaid, and even what my own inner monologue is saying. Showing up—without engagement, attention, and encouragement—is not enough.

I became a researcher because I am naturally drawn to other people's stories. The skills I've acquired have enabled me to make the space for Charlotte, and countless other participants, to be vulnerable and honest with me, a perfect stranger, about their true feelings on a variety of topics. But what I didn't know when I first started is that the skills I was learning as a researcher would serve me not just in the lab but outside of it, too. Being patient, asking open-ended questions, facilitating a conversation—these techniques help me get to the bottom of a research question, but they also help me build better relationships with my colleagues, direct reports, family, and loved ones.

Most of us listen well enough, but without deliberate attention we may move through conversation with significant blind spots. It's easy for us to learn only part of the story, or misunderstand it entirely. Miscommunication can escalate a neutral situation to a negative one, and make an already negative scenario worse. Whether our misses are big or small, when they happen, we may walk away feeling detached and isolated from others rather than connected to them. At a time when our relationships are increasingly mediated through devices that lack the warmth and honesty of a face-to-face interaction; when we are moving farther from home, and more frequently; when our social ties are weaker, our anxiety levels higher, and loneliness is on the rise; in a culture of self-promotion, overwork, and political and racial divisiveness; and in the midst of unexpected global crises that keep us not just culturally but physically far apart from each other, we need to feel connected more than ever—and listening provides a way forward.

Too often, we "solve" for miscommunication by focusing only on what we say and how we're saying it: if we could only get our message across, things would be much easier. As a result, we may decide to adjust our messaging or dial up the volume. But when we focus solely on our capabilities as speakers, we risk turning our conversation partners into an audience rather than equal collaborators. It will be hard for others to relate to us, much less put their trust in us, if that happens.

Instead, if we want to unpack others' behaviors, motivations, and the way they think about the world, listening can help get us there. When we want to hear someone's candid feelings on a topic or understand their aspirations in order to best support them, listening is what creates the space someone needs to be honest. When an argument is underway or when we engage with those who hold values or beliefs opposite to our own, thoughtful listening can help us approach them with an open mind rather than push them away. Truly effective listening can even enable others to tell us when we ourselves might be in the wrong. Every conversation is an opportunity to understand and connect with others much more deeply, if we know how to listen.

Becoming a researcher changed my approach to everyday conversation in two ways. First, I began to be more self-aware of my own listening habits, catching myself when my attention or emotions were getting in the way of my hearing others and course correcting in real time. Second, in true researcher form, I began to observe what made *others* around me effective listeners. These individuals seemed to have many of the qualities we researchers are trained in: curiosity, empathy, and the ability to ask thoughtful questions. This was a helpful observation. It suggested that the traits many of us assume to be innate—and perhaps unattainable if listening does not come to us naturally—could also be acquired.

So I began to experiment, incorporating various listening techniques into my conversations to see what worked and what didn't. Some techniques fit right into everyday conversation. Others needed minor adjustments to work in the real world, or were better for some scenarios but not others. I also discovered new techniques—techniques I would later bring back *into* my research practice. Sometimes a technique did not translate into the real world at all. And there were times when my own listening quirks would get in the way.

This book is a distillation of what I learned as I deepened my listening practice—as a user researcher and as a manager but also as a sister, daughter, wife, and friend. It is my road map to becoming a better listener, the result of many hours of conversations with strangers, expert interviews with other professional listeners, and many personal experiments, too. I hope it proves useful as you navigate the relationships in your life, whoever they're with.

If you are reading this book, chances are there is someone in your life you'd like to connect more deeply with. Perhaps you'd like to strengthen the bond between you and your partner, or deepen the ties between you and your child. Maybe you'd like to bring these skills to the workplace and utilize the power of listening to build trusting working relationships and more collaborative partnerships. Or, you may be in search of more authentic friendships than the ones you have today. Whatever your reason, I'm glad you're here. The skills we'll cover apply across these scenarios and more. With thoughtful and deliberate effort, we can be better listeners to those around us, no matter the situation.

Here's a glimpse of what's to come. In part I of this book, we'll explore the conditions for successful listening—an open mind, deliberate attention, and keen observation. In part II, we'll focus on how to best navigate the conversation as it unfolds. I'll reveal research moderating tips and tricks of the trade, like how to identify unmet needs, when and how to advance conversations, and how to create space for others to share their honest concerns, troubles, personal hopes, and dreams. And because listening can take a lot of energy, in part III, I'll share how we can support ourselves in our listening practice and recover from intense conversations.

I have been the student of many to get here: fellow researchers, therapists, coaches, journalists, and the natural-born listeners who bring empathy to the fore no matter the conversation and make up my favorite co-workers, friends, and family. Throughout this book, you'll see stories of both listening at its finest and listening gone bad in a variety of scenarios—from the research setting, to the office, to the home.

You'll also have many opportunities to put your newfound skills to practice through hands-on exercises and self-reflection prompts, and find scripts to help you go deeper in conversation. I invite you to adapt these learnings and scripts to the world *you* live in, and the unique scenarios and personalities you bring your listening practice to.

Along the way, we'll also learn a lot about ourselves. We'll bring self-awareness in to learn what our personal listening powers and pitfalls are and how to manage them. With practice, you'll begin to notice when you may be projecting your experience onto someone else's and learn to tame any instincts to interrupt, redirect, or appease others in conversation. Only in understanding ourselves can we begin to truly understand and empathize with others.

By the end of this book, I hope that you have a deeper appreciation for effective listening and an understanding of how it works—along with the support, encouragement, and practice to make it your own.

Before we get started, a note about what you're about to read: Protecting the privacy of participants is a keystone of the research practice; anonymity goes hand in hand with studies and their results. In keeping with that research tradition, any studies you read about in this book have been anonymized, meaning that I have removed or altered details to protect the identity of my subjects, the companies I've worked with, and the products they build. The stories I share blend many studies and moments from my experience as a researcher, and have been distilled here to their most essential—and, for our purposes, illuminating—form. With the exception of my interviews with experts and stories of my dear husband and me, I have taken the same approach to anonymity in the anecdotes I present in this book, whether they take place during a research session or not.

EXERCISE: **Establish Your Listening Baseline**

Throughout this book, you'll find exercises to help you practice what you're learning. To start, take this brief quiz to assess your listening skills.

1. A sibling is waxing poetic on a topic you don't care for. Do you:
   A. Check your phone
   B. Change the topic
   C. Find something you can get curious about
   D. Nod and smile

2. A partner is excited about a personal project. Do you:
   A. Tell them about a project you are excited about
   B. Start thinking about dinner
   C. Get excited with them
   D. Reaffirm they picked the right project

3. A direct report tells you they are leaving the company. Do you:
   A. Talk about how you want to leave, too
   B. Get as much information as you can on their decision
   C. Try to understand their feelings
   D. Move on to the next agenda item

4. A friend shares his relationship frustrations. Do you:
   A. Tell him you are on his side
   B. Give him advice on how to navigate his relationship
   C. Let him express himself
   D. Explain how his partner probably feels and where they might be coming from

Tally up! Did you get mostly Cs? Well done, you—you can skip to chapter 10. Mostly As, Bs, and Ds? Fear not, we are just getting started.

Part I

SET THE STAGE

CHAPTER 1

Cultivate a Listening Mindset

Eve, a young user researcher on my team, was conducting her first field study. By her side was her mentor, Mia. Their goal was to better understand the extent of cyberbullying on our platform, so that we could come up with an approach to tackle the problem. Eve and Mia would be interviewing celebrities and other public figures commonly targeted by cyberbullies "in the field," meaning outside of a lab setting, in their natural environments: on set, in the office, on the court, or even at home.

The first few interviews went smoothly. But in the third session, when a participant began to describe some of the harassment he'd faced online, Eve broke a cardinal rule of research and interrupted: "And the people who write mean things about you—you just ignore them, right?"

In qualitative research, like the study Eve and Mia were conducting, there is a saying: In the first session, you learn that not everyone is like you. In the second, you learn that not everyone is like your first participant. The rule is that only around the fifth conversation do you hear the full range of possible responses to questions and begin to see patterns in attitudinal attributes like needs, motivations, and feelings. This is why most qualitative studies involve talking to at least five participants.

Eve was repeating a sentiment she had heard participants say in her earlier interviews—that the proper response to abusive comments is to simply ignore them. But *this* participant had yet to share how he handled trolls on the platform. In addition to interrupting, Eve was basing her response on what she had heard before rather than what was right in front of her.

"Oh, actually, it kind of stings," the participant answered. "Online bullies can be hard to ignore, though it would be a lot healthier for me if I could."

Only half listening, Eve glossed over her participant's response. "Right, so you would ignore them, makes sense," she said, before moving on to the next part of the interview.

Noticing that the participant's response—and his underlying emotions—had gone unheard, her mentor, Mia, intervened. "Let's take a few steps back for a minute," she said. "What is it like to experience harassment online?" Tentatively at first, and then with vigor, the participant began to share his story.

"People think that because I'm in the spotlight I must not care what other people think—like I don't have feelings," he said. "But of course it hurts when someone says something mean about me, and especially when they attack my followers. I feel it's my responsibility to protect them, even if it hurts me."

The idea that trolling affects not just the individual but also their community was an insight we hadn't heard before, but that would become a crucial recurring theme. If Mia hadn't noticed that the participant's perspective was being ignored and stopped the conversation to get it right, then his important insight would have gone unsaid. Our product strategy—and our participants' experiences on the platform—would have suffered as a result.

We've all had conversations in which we've felt unheard, and we've all also had conversations in which we, like Eve, were the ones to miss our partner's cues and failed to truly understand them. Ineffective listening is common and happens every day. We often stop listening because we think we know what the other person is going to say (*She is so easy to read.*), because we have an informed opinion about how they will respond (*He always leads by playing devil's advocate.*), or because we have an idea of how we think they should respond (*It's obvious the correct answer is "yes."*). Sometimes we even assume our own experience is the same as others, and expect others will respond like we would (*There's no way I would take that project on given what happened the last time, and she won't either.*). But when we stop paying attention to our conversation partner and let our own thoughts and opinions run the show, we miss learning what our conversation partner really has to say. And, perhaps more importantly, we lose out on forming or strengthening a connection with that person, which can damage our relationship. This explains why some teams never seem to gel no matter how many team-building activities they try, why some siblings struggle to grow close despite their blood ties, and why even lifelong neighbors can still find themselves with little to say to one another years later. If we can't hear what others mean or how they truly feel, it will be impossible to get to know them, much less feel close to them, despite our best intentions, or even the benefits of proximity.

In order to become the listeners we aspire to be, we'll first need to distinguish what makes some kinds of listening effective and others not.

Stay Away from Surface Listening

When we, like Eve, fall into a passive state of listening, we partake in what is called *surface listening.* Surface listening is the act of hearing the literal—but not emotional—content of a conversation, often at the expense of our conversation partner's feelings. In our over-scheduled lives, surface listening is nothing if not efficient. When we are on autopilot, we hear enough of what the other person is saying to hold a conversation, get our work done, keep in touch with our friends, and stay polite with our neighbors and shopkeepers.

Unfortunately, most of us spend the majority of our time in surface listening mode. It is how we listen when we aren't paying attention. When we participate in surface listening, we tend to react based on how we wish to be treated, rather than respond to what our conversation partner is actually saying or in need of. For example, we seek to be useful, so we offer advice and problem-solve—even if our conversation partner doesn't want this. Or we wish to make others feel better, so we validate their experience—even when they don't need our words of encouragement. Other times, we seek to relate, so we share our similar stories—even though others are facing unique circumstances. And while our intentions may be good, this can cause us to miss our conversation partner's point.

One of the most common—and easiest—listening mistakes we can make in surface listening mode is to project our own feelings, ideas, or experiences onto others. We may, for instance, assume that others relate to things in the same way we do, out of a desire to bond over a "shared" experi-

PROJECTING

ence (*You had a pet as a child? Me too. It was great, right?*). But because we're usually operating within the context of our unique experiences, we risk missing signals that our perspectives may differ (*Yes, I had a cat. But it was awful—I was allergic.*).

Surface listening can also include behaviors like multitasking, interrupting others, mentally checking out, or continually bringing a conversation back to what *we* want to talk about. Being on the receiving end of these behaviors can make one feel small and lonely. When a boss fails to hear our pleas for help during a one-on-one, we may conclude that we can't ask them for support anymore. When a sibling appears distracted as we share a challenge we are going through, we may leave the conversation feeling worse than when we started. When we are excited to share a personal achievement with a spouse and they fail to acknowledge it in response, we may feel uncelebrated, even alone. Over time, such moments can start to compound and chip away at our sense of self and belonging, and we may begin to feel rejected or unworthy of being seen, heard, or appreciated for who we are.

Recognizing those moments in which we engage in surface listening is important—and lets us know that we can do better.

Embrace Empathetic Listening

To help us understand our conversation partner better, identify their needs, and decode the meaning of their unique speaking patterns and gestures, we must engage in a different form of listening. I call it *empathetic listening*, and it is this quietly powerful form of listening that we'll focus on in this book. It is what allows us to be more effective listeners, no matter the scenario.

At its core, empathetic listening is about connection. It is what happens when we deliberately slow things down and seek to understand others' inner worlds. It means taking in what another person is saying—or not saying—with the intent to understand and relate to them on a human level. When we listen with empathy, our conversation partner should feel not just comfortable but seen and known in some way. We do this by listening not just for what is said but also for what is meant—and then going deeper still to under-

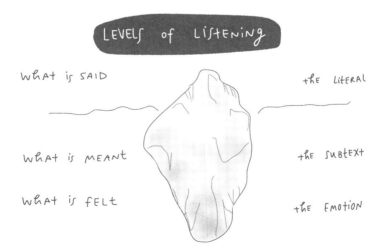

stand what is felt. With empathetic listening, it is much easier to see what our teammates need to confidently get their project over the finish line, when our partner can use our support, or when our friend must get something off his chest.

Through empathetic listening, we can create a space in which others feel safe to be themselves, laying the foundation for open and honest communication between both the speaker and the listener. This virtuous circle of connection is what I call a *listening loop*. When the loop works, we entrust our conversation partner with our emotions and make it possible for them to do the same. It feels good to go deeper in conversation and to see and hear people as they truly are, rather than as we wish them to be. The more we tune in to others, the more they tune in to us. When reciprocated, empathetic listening is the strongest salve for our sense of disconnection.

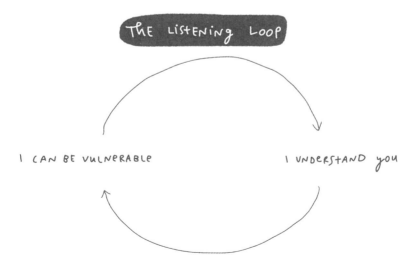

Self-Evaluate: Surface Listening or Empathetic Listening?

Assess your listening habits with the flow chart below.

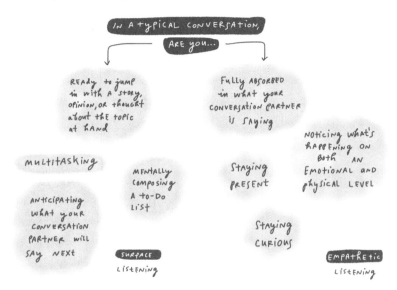

If you find you spend more time surface listening, that's OK.

In the chapters to come, we'll look at key building blocks and learn how we can strengthen our listening muscles.

If you find you spend more time empathetic listening, you're off to a great start!

Pay attention to where your natural strengths are; we'll continue to reinforce these as we practice. Note where some of the gaps might be; we'll spend time improving these, too.

If you find yourself toggling between the two, no judgment.

In later chapters, you'll learn what circumstances, company, and topics might make it harder to stay in empathetic listening mode and how to lean into it no matter the scenario.

Cultivate a Listening Mindset

Now that we can distinguish between surface listening (where many of us commonly spend our time) and empathetic listening (the most effective mode for connecting), we can begin to hone our listening practice.

To start, we must first do the work of getting into the right mindset. This means approaching a conversation with the intention to fully receive and engage with our conversation partner in an empathetic way. It means committing to meeting our conversation partner where they are, without expectations, and focusing less on our own inner narratives (and perhaps even our own needs) in the

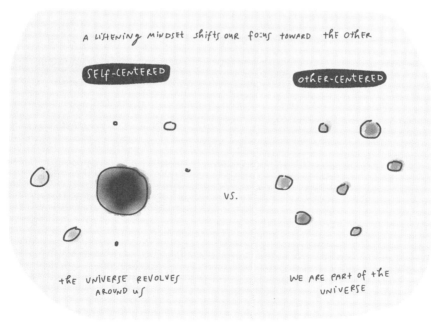

A LISTENING MINDSET shifts our focus toward the other

SELF-CENTERED

OTHER-CENTERED

VS.

the UNIVERSE REVOLVES AROUND us

WE ARE PART of the UNIVERSE

moment. Specifically, it means bringing an open mind—one of empathy (naturally), humility, and curiosity—to the conversation. Because each of these qualities asks us to shift our focus away from the self and toward the other, without this mindset, it is difficult to deliver on the promise of empathetic listening and truly connect with others.

We'll talk about each of these qualities in detail next.

EMPATHY: PUT YOURSELF IN OTHERS' SHOES

In my early days as a user researcher, I interviewed software developers about the pros and cons of using different tools on the job. On the surface, I shared almost nothing in common with the participants. Despite striving for a diversity of recruits, many fit the stereotype of software engineers in the Bay Area: often soft-spoken, introverted, and male, with hobbies like video gaming and coding. As a fairly outspoken, outgoing woman who can count on one hand the number of times she's played a video game, we were hardly an obvious match. Having experienced more than a few awkward conversations with engineers of this kind at the office, I feared our sessions would be a slog, and that our lack of chemistry might make it harder to have a rich conversation. I knew I would have to work extra hard not to let these differences derail our sessions.

Yet through empathy, I discovered ways to understand and relate to my participants. Though I wasn't familiar with the ins and outs of coding, I could appreciate their excitement at creating something out of nothing—I felt the same way at the end of a productive day of writing. I could sense their frustrations when faced with a problem they just could not solve in time, even if the details of their work were unlike anything I was personally familiar with. I could understand how gratifying it could be to finally discover the source of a problem that had left them stuck for days—a pesky bug in the code for them, or a tricky chapter structure for me. Despite our many differences, I was able to empathize with their feelings of stress, disappointment, and achievement—without making the conversation about me.

For instance, in a session, if a participant shared that a coding project was finally coming to fruition, I could ask them to say more and appreciate their journey—without sharing a similar story, giving advice, or comparing our unique experiences. Staying in their experience would allow me to ask more relevant questions. Rather than remain at the surface (*How long did the project take?*), I could tailor my approach given what I was learning (*What was it like when it all fell through? . . . And how did you recover from that? . . . What else?*). The empathy and understanding I brought to our conversation would also signal to participants that they could be honest with me (*Truthfully, it hurt to see it all fall apart.*). The more I empathized with them, the more I got to know them, the more personalized my questions became, and the more my participants opened up.

Empathy is this ability to imagine what someone might be feeling. It helps us understand how others' personal experiences and backgrounds may have shaped who they are, what they believe, and how they behave. In many ways, empathy is the antidote to projecting—we do not need to share in others' direct experience, we just need to imagine it. We can call upon our own experiences as a way to understand what others may be going through, but always keep the focus on the other person. Finding ways to personally relate—without making the conversation about us—allows us to better understand what is being said, not just at the surface level but also at the emotional level. When we practice empathy in conversation, we can get to know each other in a way otherwise inaccessible to us.

To put empathy into practice, try these tips:

- **Let others' perspectives take the lead.** Embrace the process of understanding your conversation partner's lived experience by asking questions specific to them and giving them the floor to share more.

- **Remind yourself that it's not about you.** If you find your mind wandering to, "I would have handled that differently . . ." do your best to table these thoughts. Think less about how you would have reacted if it were you and more about why your conversation partner may have made the choices he or she did.

- **Tap into their emotions.** Even if you do not have firsthand experience with your conversation partner's exact experience, try to relate to the underlying feelings that may be driving the conversation.

With empathy as our starting point, we can begin to meet others where they are in conversation.

HUMILITY: ASSUME YOU DON'T HAVE ALL THE ANSWERS

At the start of each research session, I tell my participants I am like "neutral Switzerland"—I will pass no judgment on their opinion or perspective; I want to hear it all. "You cannot hurt my feelings," I say, before inviting them to share with me the good, the bad, and the ugly. I also admit that I do not have all the answers and that I am ready to be wrong. In a way, I am asking them to be my teacher and am promising to accept and learn from the lessons they teach me.

Saying this takes only a minute but yields much more authentic responses from participants. In fact, most participants visibly relax when they hear this—they have agreed to share their opinions on a topic for an hour, without ever having met me, and sometimes without knowing what we'll be talking about or even what company I represent. Some participants may fear offending me if a design turns out to be terribly unuseful, while others may be loath to admit that they just don't understand how to use a feature. They may be so worried about saying the "wrong" thing that they stay mum altogether. Sharing my intention to practice humility in our session helps them set these concerns aside and tell me how they really feel about a product, feature, or idea. Our session goes from feeling like a test they must pass to a lesson only they have the expertise to teach.

This preamble is also an important reminder for me, as a researcher. If a participant struggles to complete a task my team believes should be a slam dunk, I know to not assume that it's "them" but instead to allow for the likely possibility that it's "us"—and do my best to understand why. A task that seems easy to us may be difficult for the participant because it was designed by someone who uses the product every day, rather than once in a blue moon, or because we've fundamentally gotten something wrong.

In a research session, my goal is not just to learn but also to be objective—but most day-to-day conversations don't come with those kinds of guardrails built in. Outside the lab, listening with humility means releasing ourselves from judgment and the assumption that we already have the answer, in order to stay open to others' ideas and opinions. It is particularly useful when we are discussing something uncomfortable, or are being criticized. With humility, we allow others to say what they need to say without fear of expressing the "wrong" thing. This allows us to be vulnerable with each other, generates intimacy between us, and can ultimately strengthen our relationships.

Without humility, we may not discover, for instance, how hard it was for our colleague to give us critical feedback, and how committed they are—despite their own discomfort—to being honest with us about something they are concerned might be holding us back. Or that our friend is not trying to pick a fight when they challenge our political views, but that their willingness to engage on this topic with us is a reflection of the deep level of trust they have in our relationship. Or that despite the heated debates and disagreement with a partner over a project we are excited about, they too share the same goal to make it the best it can be. In the absence of humility, these paths to better understanding each other would be shut.

Humility is also helpful if we find ourselves distracted by stereotypes or other assumptions that can make it hard for us to fully see and hear what is in front of us, or even blinded by our own expertise. Here our social bonds are even more at risk, since the more strongly we feel about something, the harder it is to be open to alternative points of view.

Of course, we all have limits—I am not suggesting we sit by quietly if others are offensive or go too far. Humility does not require us to reduce our point of view to a speck of dust, but it does mean being open to being wrong, and doing the very hard work of trying to understand others' perspectives. Though we may still ultimately disagree with our conversation partner—and even voice this disagreement—humility protects us from reacting prematurely. Everyone gets a chance to express their opinion.

Below are a few tips to shift your mindset to one of humility.

- **Let go of preconceived notions.** Loosen your grip on your opinions to make room for others to share their own. This allows you to hear things as they are or could be, rather than as you assume they are or wish them to be.

- **Leave judgment at the door.** Remind yourself that a difference of opinion is simply that—not better or worse, just different. This can help you stop yourself from shutting others down when they feel differently.

- **Assume you are in the presence of an expert.** Understand that others' lived experience gives them unique expertise. This can help us to accept and respect their perspective, even when it is not like our own.

CURIOSITY: BE THERE TO LEARN

For years, my user research team was responsible for ensuring that the businesses, brands, and influencers who used our platform had an amazing experience. This required us to learn what it was like to run or work for a business, and in some cases, how businesses and brands leaned on advertising to grow their reach, drive traffic to their websites, or sell their product. In truth, talking about advertising does not make my heart beat faster—but I had a job to do. I had to learn to get curious.

Getting curious means being open to learning more about a topic, idea, or person—even if it does not initially pique our interest. Though it can, at times, feel like a chore, there are many benefits to being curious. According to author and psychologist Todd Kashdan, curious people socialize better with strangers and are perceived more positively by others than incurious people. They are more likely to get along with a variety of people, and with greater social intimacy. Not only do we feel closer to curious people, but Kashdan's research even shows that we are more attracted to those who demonstrate curiosity than to those who do not.

"Being interested is more important in cultivating a relationship and maintaining a relationship than being interesting," Kashdan says. "That's what gets the dialogue going."[1] Curiosity is an invitation for others to say more in conversation—in other words, it is an olive branch for connecting.

curiosity is AN invitAtioN to CONNECt

tELL ME MoRE!   I'D LOVE +o!

In the same way, curiosity also deepens our conversations. When we demonstrate an interest in our conversation partner, we make them feel valued and thus more willing to open up, which allows us to get to know them better and more intimately. Perhaps that's why we are drawn to curious people in action, whether on talk shows or interview podcasts—they can unlock a depth of conversation and intimacy seemingly effortlessly and give us insight into others' thoughts and feelings that might otherwise be inaccessible to us.

On the flip side, when we do not demonstrate curiosity, we might inadvertently discourage our conversation partner from sharing before they have the chance to open up. You've probably felt this yourself in everyday conversations—if a colleague's eyes glaze over as you tell them about your weekend, or a friend glances at their phone while you share a personal story. Though perhaps unintentional, these reactions can feel like rejection. If it seems like your conversation partner isn't interested in what you have to say, you may begin to close the conversation: What's the point in continuing if you've lost your audience?

That's why instead of going into research sessions with advertisers assuming I'd be bored, I began to challenge myself to find an insight that could spark my curiosity. With intention, I was always able to find *something* to get curious about. Like, for instance: How confident do advertisers feel day-to-day in their decision-making? How do they stay productive despite sometimes using subpar tools? What kinds of unique pressures exist in a high-stakes, big-spending business like theirs? By finding something to be curious about, I was able to genuinely encourage my participants to share their honest experience with me, which allowed me to uncover compelling insights I could take back to my team.

EXERCISE: How Curious Are You?

Let's reflect on your baseline curiosity in conversation. Because we tend to be more curious about topics we are interested in, we'll focus on understanding your baseline when the topic is *not* one you're naturally drawn to. Consider the following scenarios:

1. At lunch, a co-worker shares a detailed account of a recent camping trip, down to the size of her hiking boots and what she ate for breakfast. You:

   A. Jump in to share your favorite breakfast spots in the city. It's not camping, but it is delicious.

   B. Mentally catalog all the chores you meant to do this weekend.

   C. Make an excuse to leave—your inbox is calling your name.

   D. Ask your colleague how she got into camping, and what she loves so much about it.

2. Your sibling is recounting his rescue dog's latest shenanigans. You:

   A. Remember a funny thing your dog did last night—and immediately tell the story.

   B. Check your phone for new notifications. Pretty sure you've heard this one before.

   C. Imagine how your dog would have behaved—she is much better trained.

   D. Listen closely to hear what new trouble his pup has gotten into. Maybe this will spark a gift idea for your brother's birthday.

3. You're at a dinner party and the conversation turns to politics. A fellow guest is eager to defend a candidate for election. You:

   A. Fact-check your dinner companion, ready to chime in with an update. Can't trust anyone's "news" sources these days.

B. Finally unsubscribe from all those promos crowding your in-box.

C. Help your host do the dishes or clear the table—anything to get out of the room.

D. Ask the guest what drew her to that candidate. You wonder what led her to support them.

If You Answered Mostly As, You Might Be a Pivoter

You have a habit of changing the conversation to make it more relevant to you. Often, you are ready to jump in with an idea, story, or correction. Since your wheels are already turning, you might miss out on what's being said.

If You Answered Mostly Bs, You Might Be a Distractor

You are a pro at finding creative ways to distract yourself from a discussion if it isn't interesting to you. As a result, you end up catching only bits and pieces of a conversation.

If You Answered Mostly Cs, You Might Be a Withdrawer

You don't care much for subtlety if a conversation isn't of interest. Your preferred strategy? Leave! And if you can't physically escape, a daydream will do the trick.

If You Answered Mostly Ds, You Might Be an Explorer

You tend to understand where others are coming from and have been known to remember the details about a person that make them unique. You are naturally positioned for empathetic listening.

BUILD YOUR CURIOSITY MUSCLE

Now that you are aware of your baseline curiosity, we'll explore how you can foster it in conversation. Because practicing curiosity is so integral to cultivating connection with others, as you'll see in the pages to come, I've devoted more time here on how best to do that. The tips below will help you get curious regardless of the scenario.

Look for Interesting Edges

My husband and I have opposite conversation styles. In a chat, he is more fact-driven and prone to googling to answer trivia or confirm a historical stat; I am more socially driven and likely to recall interpersonal details that tell me something about people and personalities. It's very easy for me to forget that the facts and stats he brings up are his way of keeping the conversation going, in the same way that when I recount an anecdote about a friend or co-worker, I am inviting him to chime in. To avoid missing each other's bids for connection, and inadvertently dismissing each other, we both have to make an effort to find interesting threads to pull.

Tugging at interesting threads in a conversation means paying attention to what's surprising or compelling to you so that you can stay engaged—and possibly even ask about it later—instead of tuning out. This is something many of us neglect to do in everyday conversation, despite having practice with it. For instance, think about all the new social situations you've encountered in your life— meeting new people, interviewing for a new job, even going on a first date—and the curiosity you displayed then, relative to your average conversation. Now, see if you can tap into that capacity for curiosity with the co-workers, friends, and family you talk to every day. Try to channel that feeling where everything is shiny, interesting, and new to you, even when it feels like a stretch. To do this, find your "in"—a thread or detail you are naturally drawn to—and seize it by asking questions like, "What was that like?," "How did you learn that?," or "Tell me more about *this* part of what you said . . ." to help you go down the rabbit hole of curiosity together.

Now when my husband brings up, for instance, basketball stats, I no longer automatically tune out. Instead, I tug at what's interesting to me and ask about the players and personalities behind the numbers. I hear about the drama, about the parties, about the coaches with interesting team traditions, like Gregg Popovich, the Spurs coach who takes his team out to Michelin restaurants after games, and about the strength and tradition of the venerable PB&J sandwich in the basketball world.[2] My husband gets to share what he knows about a favorite topic, and I get to savor the details about people along the way.

Ask: What Else?

After numerous research sessions with small business owners over the years, I can probably tell you what their primary challenges are.

I know many struggle to manage their time and may lack the resources and expertise to take their business to the next level. I also know they tend to be scrappy, entrepreneurial, and hardworking, driven by a deep commitment and enthusiasm to share their passions with others. Because I know all of this, I might be tempted to think that I don't need to interview this group anymore (*I already know what to expect.*). But if I were to stop there, I'd never deepen my knowledge of this very interesting group, and I might miss out on crucial information—and, as a result, fail to take the products we create for this group from good to great.

Instead of approaching these sessions as a checklist to confirm what I already know, I can attempt to unearth the details that will transform my general knowledge of small businesses into a richer and more nuanced understanding. For example, perhaps I know time is a scarce resource for small business owners. But what exactly do their daily schedules look like? How do they manage the busiest days of the year, like Small Business Saturday, relative to an average or even a slow day? What emotional impact do milestone moments like these have on them?

By remaining curious even when we have a strong baseline of knowledge, we can deepen our expertise and in turn better get to know others. If you are well versed in a topic, don't stop there. Instead, ask yourself: What details might I be missing? What else can I learn? How might my understanding of this subject be incomplete?

Discover the Why

A colleague once scheduled a meeting to discuss what a team should be called. "The team has too many names and it's confusing to everyone involved," she explained. She reserved thirty precious minutes for five managers to pick a new name and discuss how it should be rolled out in the organization.

My first instinct was: this is not a good use of time. Why pull this many busy people into a room to create a naming convention for a team we aren't even on?

But then I stopped myself and got curious. What was driving this conversation? Why was my co-worker so passionate about something as seemingly trivial as a team name? Through careful observation and a few pointed questions (*What outcome are you working toward? How would you prioritize this against other tasks on our plate?*), I learned that, for her, it is *extremely* important that her direct reports have a shared understanding of a team's goals, processes, and, yes, even their name. In the end, I could agree with the spirit of her argument—the importance of clarity to enable great work—even if I hadn't at first understood her intentions or her approach.

This was a helpful learning in the moment but also for the future. When a conflict between two of our direct reports surfaced later on, I remembered this particular manager was driven by process and clarity above all. So instead of focusing on why these two specific individuals were not partnering well, I framed the situation as an example of how our teams could collaborate more closely—if only we had a shared framework and set of best practices for how they should partner together. In emphasizing the need for clarity and alignment, I made it easy for her to genuinely want to partner with me. Because of this, together, we not only addressed the conflict between our two reports but tightened the partnership between our teams overall.

What can a person's choice of topic tell you about *them*? Getting curious about why *this* person is so drawn to *this* topic helps us silence our old friend, projection. The following thought starters can help:

- How important does this subject seem to my conversation partner?

- Which part of our conversation are they particularly passionate about? Not passionate about?

- What might be driving their [enthusiasm, frustration, disappointment] for this topic? Could there be an emotional, contextual, personal, or even historical reason for their choice of topic?

- What might be motivating their reaction to what's been said? Might their personal history play a part?

Prepare Yourself

The older we get, the more distinct our tastes, preferences, and interests can become. There's nothing wrong with not being curious about certain topics—you can honor your selective interests and still show up for others.

Instead of dreading conversations about topics you're not particularly interested in, or with people with whom you have little in common, you can proactively combat boredom with a simple pep talk. First, acknowledge that this conversation isn't interesting to you, whether you're listening to your co-worker talk about the latest biography she's reading, a genre of book you have never voluntarily picked up, going deep with your nephew on the intricacies of science fiction characters you've never heard of, or talking politics at a dinner party when you'd rather not, thank you very much. Then, tell yourself something like: *This may not be my favorite subject, but I can handle it.* Or, *This might be a boring topic, but I can manage this.* From there, challenge yourself to stay active and alert in the conversation you're in, rather than playing it easy and zoning out.

BEFORE YOU FORGET

The easiest place to be in conversation is in our own heads—judging, assuming, and projecting our experience onto others. The best way to get out of this kind of surface listening is to put yourself in other people's shoes, stay humble, and get curious. Bringing these qualities into conversation sets us on the path to connection.

CHAPTER 2

Stay Present

For months, Fran and Marcus had been itching to conduct a joint research project on the future of travel that would combine each of their superpowers—survey design for Fran and in-depth interviews for Marcus. It was a dream that had been neglected given competing priorities, until finally, the business was ready for it.

It was a Monday morning, and at their first project meeting, Fran was energetic and ready to get started. She had put together an agenda for their time together and began to tick items off one by one.

"Let's start with scope. This project could get very knotty very fast if we're not careful," she said. "One option is for us to take a multiphased approach, organized by modes of transportation: air travel first, then car, train, bike, and by foot." Marcus yawned and nodded. "Or, we could design it according to why people travel: business travel first, then leisure travel after," she suggested. "Mm-hmm,"

Marcus said, stirring his coffee. "Or maybe by methodology? Large-scale survey first to get a holistic view of the market, then in-depth interviews to follow," she said. "Could be," Marcus said.

Fran struggled to make sense of her colleague's monotone reactions but pressed on. But as Marcus's responses remained unchanged, Fran began to lose confidence. "Marcus," Fran said, slowly closing her laptop. "Is this project going to be a priority for you? I was really excited about this and thought you were, too, but I'm a little confused. I feel like I'm on my own here."

"I'm sorry," Marcus said. "I promise I am all in on this project. I am just really not a morning person."

That was a lightbulb moment for Fran. The problem was not that Marcus was disinterested; it was that at that moment, he was having trouble staying present. At 9 A.M. on a Monday, they were each simply on opposite wavelengths. Fran was relieved and could relate to feeling so exhausted you are on autopilot—it was exactly how *she* felt most afternoons—and how being tired physically, but especially mentally and emotionally, can make it difficult to stay present. Together, Fran and Marcus learned that to get the connection they were both seeking, they should schedule their meetings in that late morning, early afternoon window when they would both be ready to go.

Staying present is essential for empathetic listening to occur. When we are present, we are able to take in more information about our partner—what they are saying or even nonverbally suggesting—that lets us in on what they are actually feeling. In a group, we can begin to observe the power dynamics and subtle cues that indicate tacit agreement, confusion, and even the simmering tension beneath the surface that can later turn into disagreement. One-on-one, we can train our attention on the unique gestures, fleeting hesitations, and even the melody of what our conversation partner is saying. When we are attuned in this way, we are able to better grasp what our partner really needs. Our conversation partners, in turn, can feel our efforts—in the warmth of our attentiveness, the commitment to hearing them out, our dedication to staying with them despite other distractions—and respond in kind. In this way, staying present can help our conversation partners to feel cared for, valued, and tended to, which encourages them to share what's on their mind.

Staying present has other benefits, too, like helping us to avoid the "Huh?" moments that may make us look unserious or even incompetent at our job. We needn't worry about saying, "What's that, again?" when we're present, which can make us appear unfocused or even self-centered in the presence of our loved ones. Nor must we grasp at straws to explain why we are distracted (*Sorry! I was just, um, checking what time it was?*), since we are no longer at risk of being caught with our minds elsewhere.

When we are not present, we may make little progress on a problem, answer the wrong question, misinterpret our partner's position, or, as with Marcus and Fran, risk making others feel rejected. We may also quickly make missteps, like jumping ahead and telling others what we think they want to hear, instead of hearing them out and truly getting to know them. Do this once and we miss an opportunity to understand our conversation partner; do this repeatedly and we begin to appear disinterested, unreliable, impatient, even dismissive. When this happens, our conversation partners may begin to hold back. As a result, our conversations can feel like a struggle, or even a grind, instead of an opportunity for connection.

There is no quicker way to end a conversation—or a relationship—than to appear distracted.

There are three skills that allow us to stay present as we listen, each of which builds upon the other and requires mindfulness, the ability to be aware of what is happening in a given moment.

Self-Awareness helps us know what each of us personally needs to stay present so that we can be there for others in conversation.

Trust allows us to stay in the moment and receive others with ease rather than worry we will forget something important or miss our conversation partner's point.

Patience helps us to slow down our response and make space for others to finish their thoughts or take their time to process or sit with what's been said.

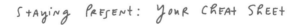

STAYING PRESENT: YOUR CHEAT SHEET

PATIENCE — REMEMBERING to cool our JETS

TRUST — KNOWING the important stuff WILL RETURN

AWARENESS — noticing our flawed attention span

mindfulNESS — the foundation for ALL progress

Self-Awareness

It was my third back-to-back one-on-one of the day, and my brain was quickly frying. In my quest to be efficient, I had scheduled myself into a corner, and now my attention was suffering. With each conversation, I dropped into a new world of unique challenges, personalities, and details to absorb.

Now, Lily, a junior researcher on my team, was updating me on a project she was having trouble with. She was planning a large-scale study for the first time and having a hard time recruiting the right participants. As she dove into the details of her problem, I found myself struggling to keep up. All I could think of was my previous meeting. A direct report had shared some serious hurdles he was facing with his stakeholders, and I found myself continuing to turn over his challenge in my mind, mentally playing out possible solutions.

"So what do you think I should do?" Lily asked me. I could not for the life of me remember where we had left off.

"Walk me through your initial thinking," I said, since I generally try to coach more than direct my team, and this could also buy me more time to understand Lily's issue.

"Like I said, this one is so tricky I'm not even sure where I should start," she said. Oops, two strikes on my part—it seemed we had covered this same ground earlier, while my mind was elsewhere. The stresses of my previous conversation had spilled over, and my thoughts, I had to acknowledge, had begun to wander on their own. I was guilty of distraction, and Lily could have been annoyed or upset with me; if she felt unsupported, I wouldn't have blamed her. Realizing this, I became more motivated to bring myself back to—and stay in—the present. I didn't want Lily to feel like I wasn't taking her seriously, or that I didn't find her work interesting or important. I didn't want to risk losing her trust, either, or giving her the wrong advice.

I reeled myself back in, aware of how quickly I'd failed to be fully present for Lily. *OK*, I thought to myself, *focus*. "Sorry," I admitted aloud, "I think I lost you on that one. Take me back a few steps?" Luckily, Lily was understanding and retold her story. This time, when a thought about my previous one-on-one intruded, I mentally pushed it aside. With a few minutes of focused attention, I started to understand that Lily's problem was not her recruiting plan but her stakeholders' perception of it. "They don't understand how hard I'm working to get things done behind the scenes," she said. With deliberate attention, our conversation became much more productive.

Building awareness of my meandering thoughts allowed me to tune in to what Lily was really experiencing—not the bits and pieces I had gathered in between distractions, or her literal recounting of the story, either. From there, I was able to uncover the root cause of her problem and the true source of her stress, which made our time together more effective and our working relationship stronger. I didn't have to worry about letting Lily down, solving the wrong problem, or damaging our relationship.

In the same way, being *self-aware* as we listen is crucial to showing up for our partner and hearing and making sense of what they have to say. When we bring awareness to our listening experience, we can also better manage our response if and when we do get off track. Understanding ourselves allows us to be there for others.

Here are some tips to bolster your self-awareness and rein in wandering thoughts to stay present.

NAME WHAT IS HAPPENING

The simple exercise of recognizing my experience with Lily for what it was—stress, distraction, and concern over my previous conversation—helped me come back to the present to address her actual challenges.

Psychologists call this practice *labeling* or *naming*: we specify the emotion we are feeling in order to more effectively manage it. When we articulate what is happening, we give ourselves a choice in how to respond. This technique is especially effective when what is preventing us from staying present is the intensity of our emotions. If, for instance, we find ourselves in a stressful situation, telling ourselves things like "This is my anxiety speaking" or "I am having a strong reaction to what's happening" can help us return to the present. Labeling emotions can provide clarity in the moment (*That's my fear rearing its ugly head.*) and control (*This fear comes from my overactive imagination, and I don't need to pay it mind right now.*). This process helps us gain distance from what we are feeling and regulate our emotions in real time.[1]

You can employ labeling not just for managing strong emotions in the moment, like when we are in the face of anxiety, but also for managing thoughts that are rote, neutral, or nonemotional, such as ruminating on a prior one-on-one, as I was, or running through to-do lists, weighing possible dinner plans, making observations about your present environment, or anything else that prevents you from being fully present while listening. If you notice your mind wandering, acknowledge this by naming what is happening. This can be as simple as saying to yourself: "There goes my mind wandering again" or "It looks like my thoughts are starting to run the show." Then, send them off for good measure with a "Thanks for the visit, but you can go now" or "I am ready to move on" to help concentrate your attention back on your partner.

When we name our wandering thoughts for what they are, we can choose what to do with them. Do we need these thoughts interrupting this moment? Are they serving us in conversation, or are they merely a distraction? If the latter, we can ask our thoughts to hold tight until we're ready for them.

TUNE IN TO YOUR BODY

Sometimes what is happening in our bodies is easier to name than what is happening in our minds. Tuning in to our physical experience can give us valuable clues about whether we are in a space to truly stay present with our conversation partner.

If I know I am going into a performance review or conversation about a hot button topic where I am at risk of getting defensive or emotionally charged, I will take extra care to tune in to my body both before and during the conversation.

For example, am I boxing myself in, pinning my arms across my chest, with my legs crossed tightly beneath me? This is a position of protection, not compromise. Am I sitting as far away as possible from my conversation partner? I'm never going to get over a fight with my friend if I keep them at arm's length. Am I taking short or deep breaths? If I am not relaxed, it will be harder to focus on what the other person has to say. Am I avoiding eye contact like the plague? I may be shirking responsibility for my role in conversation. Am I shaking my head from side to side? I may be saying no before hearing the other person out.

| RECEPTIVE VERSUS PROTECTIVE POSTURES ||
Receptive Postures	Protective Postures
Arms open, uncrossed, or outstretched	Arms crossed
Feet facing our conversation partner	Feet pointing toward an exit
Regular eye contact	Minimal eye contact

When we can identify what's happening in our body, we can better manage our response. We can uncross our arms and open ourselves up to the moment, releasing tension that may be distracting us and signaling to our conversation partner that we are ready to receive more. We can deepen our breathing and slow down our pulse rate when we are in a high-alert state. We can train our eyes back to our conversation partner if we find we have been looking away. In becoming more physically receptive to our conversation partner, we become more open to hearing what they need to say. In times when we can't control our thoughts, we can control our body to help us return to the present.

EXERCISE: Try a Body Scan

Tune in to what's happening in your body by conducting a body scan. A body scan is a quick check-in to bring awareness to any tension in your body. Starting at your toes and moving up to the top of your head, focus your attention on each part of your body. Notice where you are holding tension, and where you feel relaxed. Ask yourself: What emotional responses might explain what I am feeling? Now, focus your breathing on each part of your body and notice what changes with each inhale and exhale. Follow your breath to release any tension and encourage relaxation. Use this practice to help center yourself every day, and especially before having difficult conversations.

SET YOURSELF UP FOR SUCCESS

My five-year-old pup, Moose, is a rescue dog. As with most rescues, he is adorable but also unpredictable. Over time, we've learned that there are certain stimuli that Moose simply can't handle: older gentlemen with glasses, dogs so large they look like bears, and a certain neighbor's dog who gleefully barks at our door three times a day. (It's a long story.) When Moose encounters these stimuli, he 100% loses it. All the dog training we've worked on? Completely out the window. The promise of a treat for good behavior? Irrelevant. In these moments, Moose becomes what trainers call "over threshold"—he can no longer behave rationally, much less hear us. As soon as these stimuli disappear, however, he is back to his normal, pleasant self.

It turns out humans can be over threshold, too: certain conditions can throw us off our game and make it harder to stay present and have the productive, empathetic conversations we seek. In addition to learning how to manage our behavior in the moment, ideally, we can prevent ourselves from getting thrown off in the first place. To do this, we have to take what we know about ourselves—the stimuli that bring out the worst in us, as well as the conditions that keep us calm, satisfied, and on our best behavior—and design an environment that best supports our needs. Below are a few tips for how to identify what you need to stay present and create the right environment to do so.

Manage Your Energy

One of the key ingredients to managing your focus in conversation is to ensure you have the energy to take on the work of staying present. Here, there are many potential detractors to be aware of.

Take food, for instance. We know meals have an impact on our energy level and thus our ability to stay present—whether we're distracted by hunger, energized by a snack break, or sleepy after a big meal.

Time of day can also act as an inhibitor to staying present. If you've ever given a presentation late in the day or sat through one yourself, you know how hard it can be to fight the afternoon slump, no matter how interesting the topic. Many, including your audience, are likely to be more alert and engaged earlier in the day. Of course, this is variable depending on the person, as we saw with

Fran and Marcus, but some trends are common. For example, a 2011 study published in the *Proceedings of the National Academy of Sciences* found that court sentences at the start of the day and just after a judge's lunch break were much more likely to be favorable than those at any other time of the day—probably because these judges were well caffeinated, well fed, and fresh from a break.[2] Trials that took place at the end of the day, when energy levels were more likely to be lower, received reduced rates of clemency.

The ultimate culprit for energy depletion—and thereby our inability to stay present—is, of course, sleep. Research shows that when we are sleep-deprived, the amygdala, the fight or flight region of the brain, kicks into high gear.[3] This is why exhaustion makes us more likely to pick fights and focus on negative experiences than positive ones.

OUR ENERGY LEVELS CAN MAKE OR BREAK

OUR ABILITY to STAY PRESENT

FULL BATTERY = GOOD CHANCE　　LOW BATTERY = LOW CHANCE

Find Your Zone

Hunger, time of day, and lack of sleep may be some of the most common culprits that prevent us from being present while listen-

ing, but there are other factors that can affect each of us individu-
ally. While one person may find it energizing to spend time with a
friend at a concert, another might find that environment draining
and prefer a quieter place to talk. One friend might have no problem staying present through back-to-back social events, and another may be tuckered out after the first party. Make sure you know
what you need in order to be present in conversation, and be strategic about what your conversation partner might need, too. This can
be as simple as asking your team if they are early birds or night owls
before scheduling that 9 A.M. meeting, noticing if your spouse finds
the same enjoyment in a dinner date after a long day at the office as
you do or prefers something like a weekend walk instead, and even
making note of how certain environments, like malls, parks, cities,
and countryside, affect others' moods the next time we hope to go
deep with them.

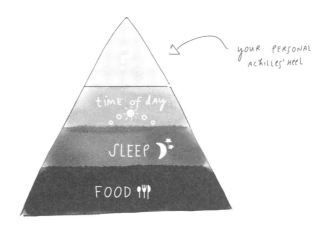

HIERARCHy of NEEds to stAying PREsENt

Free Yourself of Distractions

Finally, though we may believe we are superheroes capable of juggling everything at once, in order to stay truly present in conversation, we will have to let this belief go. Context switching, multitasking, and juggling other distractions can seriously hinder our ability to stay present. Do your best to put your phone and other distraction culprits away, and try not to schedule important conversations back-to-back, as I failed to do with Lily and my team. It takes our brains a minute to process what we've experienced before we can switch gears and do the difficult but necessary work of staying present.

Things that impact our ability to stay present

time of day

context switching

devices

appetite

energy

environment

To manage our energy levels and the stimuli that may inhibit us from staying present in conversation, try the following:

- **Fill up the tank.** Don't show up hungry to a friend's party or empty-handed to a daylong work offsite—only your host knows how much food they'll have on hand when you get there. Just as you would prepare for a long hike, if you have a lengthy meeting or marathon social event to attend, pack snacks to keep energy levels up so you can focus on your conversation partner, not your tummy.

- **Healthy body, focused mind.** Prioritize your well-being to help you to be your best self and stay present. Don't power through a cold at work, and get regular, restful sleep. There are no points for showing up too exhausted to listen; aim to take care of yourself first in order to be there for others.

- **Catch yourself—and others—in their prime.** If you're having a tête-à-tête, do so when you and your conversation partner are free from distractions—not while you are watching TV or cooking, for instance, or when they are faced with a stressful deadline and likely to be drained.

EXERCISE: Conduct an Energy Audit

What conditions must be met in order for you to stay present in conversation? To find out, notice your energy levels throughout the day. Pay attention to when you space out, get distracted, or let your mind wander in conversation. At the end of the day, ask yourself these questions to help you identify any patterns:

- When was I zoning out or distracted?
- When did I have great focus?

- What topics left me feeling great?
- What topics left me feeling exhausted?
- Whose company energized me?
- Whose company drained me?

Reflecting on your responses, what conditions enable you to be fully present and engaged while listening?

PUNT IF YOU NEED TO

If, despite your best intentions to orchestrate the right conditions, you find yourself unable to stay present and be the empathetic listener your conversation partner deserves, postponing your conversation may be your best bet. The most effective way to do this is to be honest: share why you'd like to table your chat and offer an alternative. For instance, you might say:

- I want to make sure I'm operating at 100% for our chat. Let's talk in the morning, when I'm likely to be freshest.

- Discussing this is important to me, but I can feel myself fading fast. I need a snack and then I'll be able to focus. Mind moving this conversation to a café with me?

- I've learned that too many social outings leave me zapped, and I've already had three today. OK if we meet tomorrow instead? Some solo time will help me recharge for our conversation.

- I want to give this the attention it deserves, but I am so freaking tired. Can I call you after I nap?

Trust

During a research session, everything a participant says is potentially important. As a researcher, it can be tempting to want to transcribe every story shared, observation made, insight revealed, or even bud of inspiration as it happens in real time. But taking notes can be problematic—not only does it create a barrier between us and the participant, who may now begin to wonder what it is we are writing, and why, and possibly even if they are answering "correctly"—but it also makes it virtually impossible to keep listening. The minute our pen hits the page, we lose out on what's happening at that moment.

That's part of why researchers typically record their sessions—there is no need to write down every detail when you know you can go back to it later. At the same time, many researchers will tell you that those recordings aren't actually necessary—a successful session leaves a researcher clear-eyed about what they've heard, without having to return to it. The real purpose of these recordings, I think, is to provide reassurance: in a session, they allow us to stay calm. When we don't have to worry about missing something our participant has said, or work hard not to forget an idea sparked by something we've heard, we can concentrate on what we're hearing and give others our full attention.

Whether in a meeting, over dinner, at home, or in the office, many of our conversations come with a fear of missing out. Not the Instagram kind of FOMO but the kind where we worry that we'll miss something important, whether it's a detail our conversation partner mentions, a thought of our own that we believe is worth holding on to, or next steps from a meeting that are crucial to follow through on. To alleviate the fear that we won't hear it all or remember it if we do, instead of hitting "Record" like researchers do, we may jot down a note mid-conversation (*Let me add that to my list of to-do's real quick.*), shoot off an email in real time (*Before I forget!*), or even mentally "transcribe" a plan or chore our conversation partner has reminded us of by repeatedly turning it over in our mind (*The book she just mentioned would make a great gift for her birthday next month!*).

But sometimes, the same techniques that help us feel engaged or even productive can get in the way of our ability to stay present and put a wedge between us and our conversation partner. When we are too busy trying to remember or not miss a thing, we may get so caught up in our efforts that we can no longer take in what others are saying. To our conversation partner, this may look like less eye contact, more interruptions, and a growing doubt that we are with them at all. In a research session, during a one-on-one meeting, or even a job interview, this behavior can be very disconnecting.

If self-awareness helps us to understand ourselves in order to be there for others, *trust* helps us to quiet our impulse to do more than just be present. Often, when we think of trust, we think of trust between people or within groups. But we can also put trust in ourselves: to have faith that we will remember what is necessary, to have confidence that we will pay attention to the right cues, to let go of the anxiety that we will forget an important insight and not worry, because we trust that we've got this. When we can embrace an attitude of trusting that what is important will remain with us—that no immediate action is necessary—we can stay calm and simply listen. As a result, our conversations go much further: we hear more of what *actually* matters because we are not weighed down by what *could* matter. We needn't worry about missing a key point in conversation and can spend that energy staying present instead. We'll learn how to do this next.

PINPOINT THE EMOTIONS

Rather than attempt to retain every word our partner says, we can aim to understand the gist, or overall idea, to help us stay present in conversation. That means letting distracting details go to make space for greater understanding. For instance, in a lab session, I might focus on learning whether a participant grokked a prototype or was confused by it, or whether they found it easy to use or difficult, and why—without trying to note every click, tap, sigh, or exact voice-over in real time. This is easier than it sounds, thanks to what is known as the verbatim effect of memory, so-called because it is much easier to remember the gist than it is to remember exact verbiage (the verbatim). Put another way, we naturally remember meaning better than details, and meaning, for our purposes, exists in empathy—in sensing the feelings, beliefs, and experiences of others. Luckily for us, the brain remembers emotions quite well—better than details.[4]

You've likely experienced this yourself before; the more things resonate on a human or emotional level, the more likely you are to remember them. Marriage vows, political campaign promises, your company's annual hiring plan—the details are much harder to retain (and often less crucial) than remembering the underlying emotion (that a friend is in love, that an acquaintance is excited by a particular candidate, that your CEO is worried about having enough resources). Similarly, when we can step back from the minutiae of a co-worker's update on a project to see that they are overwhelmed, or get past the details of a sibling's intense workweek to hear that they are stressed, we are not likely to forget our conversation. How someone feels is much harder to forget than the exact words they speak in the moment.

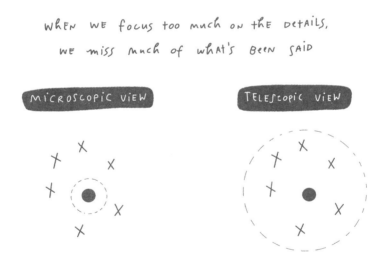

So cut yourself some slack, and don't try too hard to memorize things word for word. Instead, you can trust your human heart and intuitive memory to help you remember what's important.

SET ASIDE TIME FOR LATER

Of course, in any given conversation, we may still find interesting details we wish to hold on to. When this happens, we may once more be tempted to write things down or even mentally record them in our minds. But at the risk of missing out on what's important because you're too busy cataloging what's happening now for later, your best bet is to set aside time to capture these details after your conversation instead. Try reserving time immediately following your conversation to briefly jot down your thoughts, or even debrief with a friend or teammate while the specifics are still fresh. Since you'll naturally remember the overall idea, a few minutes should do the trick. Knowing that you have that time set aside in advance can help you engage in uninterrupted conversation, without becoming stressed mid-chat. This process works particularly well when you are working hard not to miss something your conversation partner is saying.

TAKE YOUR THOUGHTS LESS SERIOUSLY

Sometimes it is *our* idea—not our conversation partner's—that we want to hold on to. We may not want to lose the thread of a promising thought or interesting idea during a rich discussion, forget a to-do that has just come to mind, or neglect a personal revelation that surfaces in the midst of an inspiring conversation. Such thoughts can feel crucial to address at that moment. But if we believe that every thought we have during a discussion is essential, it will be impossible to stay present for our conversation partners.

In fact, most of our thoughts are little more than a distraction.

While some of the ideas we work hard to hold on to may be worth returning to, like an exciting solution to a problem you have been noodling on, or a spark of inspiration for a new recipe you'd like to try, many are often little more than humble reminders for tasks that can wait, like mentally drafting an email, making a grocery list, and other minor distractions that somehow popped into our brain during conversation.

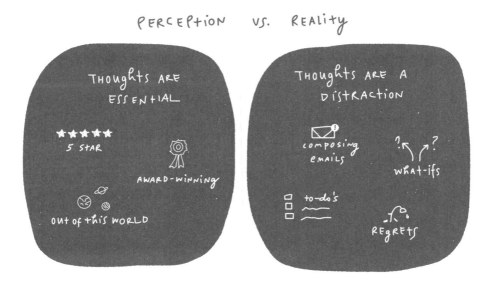

While it's natural for thoughts to run through our heads in conversation, we don't have to give them free rein. If we remember that not every thought is essential, we can free ourselves from their strong hold on our attention. Releasing our thoughts helps us to stay present with our conversation partner so we can understand their perspective and hear ideas we may not have gotten to by ruminating on our own.

When a thought arises and we're tempted to let it steal the show, we can reassure ourselves with a mantra: *If it's really that important, it will come back to me.* Typically, it does.

EXERCISE: Evaluate Your Thoughts

Try this brief meditation exercise to understand your thought patterns and when they are preventing you from staying present.

- Find a tranquil place free of distractions and set a timer for a few minutes. Close your eyes and begin to quiet your mind.
- Observe every thought that comes to mind without judgment. There is no right or wrong number of kind of thoughts to have.
- Release each thought as it enters. If you find yourself returning to a thought, wanting to hold on to it, or even deepen it, simply notice that, and move on.
- When your timer sounds, quickly capture each fleeting thought on paper.
- Review your list of thoughts. What is actually as essential as it felt in the moment? What, upon second glance, is, in fact, trivial?

For most of us, the majority of the thoughts on our list will likely be nonessential. This is natural. Our minds have a lot to say, but these thoughts don't always need to be prioritized. Freeing, isn't it?

EMERGENCY EXCEPTIONS

On rare occasions, we do need to address a thought as soon as it arises. Maybe you realize you never signed that permission slip, and your son's field trip is today. Or your manager reminds you that it's your new hire's first day at the office and you might want to show them to their desk ASAP.

When a thought cannot wait, it may be best to address the matter head-on. Gently let your conversation partner know where your thinking is, and how a brief pause will allow you to get back to your conversation with conviction. Phrases like, "I just realized that . . . Let me make this call so I can be more present for this" or "I completely forgot that . . . Let me quickly jot this down so I can focus on you instead of trying to remember that . . ." can help. This way, you avoid completely ignoring your conversation partner or becoming so distracted that you cannot hear them at all.

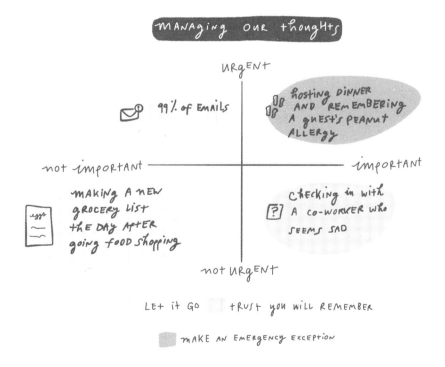

Remember to be judicious with how often you break for an emergency in conversations. Be honest with yourself about what constitutes an emergency and what does not. Take these breaks only when necessary, lest your conversation partner start to think of you as forever distracted or rarely reliable.

Patience

Early in my career I noticed that in team meetings, whenever a manager or team lead posed a question to the group, I was quick to offer an answer. Perhaps because I grew up with three sisters, I was accustomed to speaking up in group settings and had no qualms about competing for airtime. I also wanted to get things done as efficiently as possible, so if a topic needed discussion or a problem needed brainstorming, what better way to keep things moving along than to weigh in with ideas? Though I was always ready to contribute, I was also aware that there were people on my team who *never* spoke up.

One such teammate was Diego, a bright, recent grad six months into his first industry job who was as sharp as a tack but rarely contributed in meetings. Eventually, I began to wonder if my willingness to jump in first in conversations might be making it harder for co-workers like him to participate. Over time, I began to peel back and force myself to *not* be the first person to chime in. Sometimes, I silently followed the second hand on the clock to keep myself busy. Other times, I'd avoid eye contact with my manager so I wouldn't feel guilty about letting her question hang in silence. It made for some awkward moments in the beginning, but it also worked. Diego began to speak up more.

Seeing Diego come out of his shell was exciting, but even more rewarding was learning from him. Because he was new to the tech scene and an expat, his reference points were refreshingly unique. As a result, he contributed far more out-of-the-box ideas and creative solutions than many of the more tenured staff. Over time, with the space to speak up in group meetings, he became a valued member of our team.

If trust helps us to more fully receive what others have to say, *patience* is what we offer in return. The two are closely related, since both ultimately enable us to hear what our conversation partners have to say. But a lack of patience can heighten the stakes, making it that much harder to connect with others. Whether we are eager to contribute our ideas, striving toward efficiency, certain about how to proceed, feeling pressured to participate, or simply enthusiastic to connect, by giving others the space to express themselves, we not only get to know them better, but we are more likely to respond in a way that deepens the conversation. We may discover, for instance, that we can be most valuable as a sounding board, or most effective as a coach, guide, advocate, or even challenger of others' ideas. We may find that our conversation partner has everything they need to come to their own conclusion, or, on the contrary, that they need more information to come to a decision. And in group settings, being patient allows us to take in a range of perspectives to inform our position, which helps us to collaborate better and come to the best decision for the group.

Here are some techniques to try when you are in need of a dose of patience.

WIND DOWN, NOT UP

What really helped me slow my roll in group meetings was to remind myself to wind down, not wind up: whenever a thought or possible response entered my mind, rather than weighing in immediately, I simply observed it instead.

I began doing this after consulting with Christine Perry, a life coach and expert listener based in Silicon Valley who regularly brings mindfulness practices into her coaching. She encourages her clients to tune in to the present to help them build relationships and influence in the workplace. "Mindfulness is being present to what's happening in the room," she told me. "Instead of being ready to be on the fence, or coming up with what we need to say, we're just there absorbing so that we can be flexible, calm, and more responsive in the conversation."

We can practice mindfulness by observing our thoughts without letting them run the show. When we are able to put aside planning for the "right" response or stop listening to our own narratives—what we believe, assume, or desire to be true—we can better focus on what our partners are actually saying in the moment. To wind down in conversation, observe thoughts as they come, let them through without judgment, and remind yourself to return to the present.

WAIT AND SEE

Sometimes we are quick to respond to what's been said, and sometimes it hasn't even been said yet.

Years ago, I conducted a research study that brought my team into participants' homes to observe how they cooked everyday meals. I was interested to see how they incorporated both the new (mobile apps, voice-activated timers, and the like) and the old (cookbooks, recipe clippings, and even their good old-fashioned memory) into their cooking process.

There were many times when I noticed something and immediately wanted to ask about it. Did the participant often follow the recipe on the back of the pasta box? Did they feel confident in their ability to sear that steak? Were they worried about timing? Did they take any shortcuts? But if I had asked these questions in the moment, I would have missed out on potentially important information. At best, I would have interrupted their flow and overlooked a crucial step. At worst, I might have biased them to a particular technique, made them nervous, or even inadvertently caused them to change their process and "perform" for me based on what they thought I wanted to see.

In research, the stakes are high: if I interrupt a participant, I may never get back the opportunity to learn what they actually wanted to say or do. Do this one too many times, and I risk biasing the data altogether. So whenever I had a burning question, I'd wait to see if their actions could answer it for me instead. By sitting tight and quietly observing them, I could quickly tell whether a participant was struggling to get a recipe right or cooking with ease, and even gusto. Instead of asking where their recipes came from, I could watch as they passed over cookbooks for their favorite cooking app. By being a fly on the wall, I learned more than I ever could from asking a question directly.

When you are desperate to weigh in, consider what information you might miss by doing so. Take a time-out and simply wait. Count to ten and see what you can learn by staying present and observing. If this feels impossible, I find that creating a physical restriction like sitting on your hands, wriggling in your seat, or even giving yourself a teeny, tiny pinch if need be can also help pass the time as you pause.

FORGET MIND-READING

People say that when you're close to someone, you can finish each other's sentences—twins, siblings, even some couples are said to have this power. I sometimes feel like this when my husband and I are talking. He'll be analyzing something he read in the paper, and I'll jump in excitedly to finish his thought, only to have him stop and correct me: "That's actually not what I was going to say." Oops!

Attempting to finish other people's sentences may be our way of bidding for connection, but it rarely gets us there. We may jump in because we are excited to engage with others, or to show how well we know the other person, but we can miss that our conversation partner hasn't finished what they need to say. This type of behavior can be hurtful for those on the receiving end (*You must not value my opinion if you are so quick to cut me off.*), especially if we think we know where our conversation partner is going and get it wrong (*You thought I meant what? I guess you don't know me at all.*). It can even cause the other person to shut down entirely ("Never mind" is the kiss of death in my house). If this happens, you may have to work hard to coax out what someone wanted to say—or admit that they no longer want to say it.

To quell your impulse to complete your conversation partner's thought, do your best to remind yourself that everyone processes information and emotions differently and at their own pace. Your conversation partner may still be working on a thought, if you give them a beat to share it. Plus, your assumption as to what they're about to say may be wrong. The next time you feel compelled to finish their thoughts, remember what's at stake. Are you comfortable with potentially pushing your conversation partner away?

BEFORE YOU FORGET

When we stay present while listening, we invite our conversation partners to share their experience, perspective, and feelings with us without interruption or distraction. This allows us to learn about them—how they think and feel, and what makes them unique—and from them, too. By being aware of our wandering thoughts, trusting in our memory, and practicing patience, we can show up for our conversation partner in the same way we'd like them to show up for us. Invest in your relationships by noticing when you become distracted and cooling your jets when your thoughts come into the picture. Above all, focus.

CHAPTER 3

Observe as You Listen

Anyone who has ever worked with self-reported data knows it may be flawed, because it comes from humans. Just think back to all the times your doctor has asked you about your drinking habits at your annual physical—have you ever fibbed in response (*Do I really drink three glasses of wine a night? That's embarrassing. Let's call it one glass instead.*)? For this reason, in user research, we learn to not always take participants' answers literally, lest we confuse someone's intent, aspiration, or impression (*I exercise every day.*) with their reality (*I have a gym membership that I feel guilty about not using.*). Instead, we take self-reported data from surveys or interviews and pair it with observed data (derived from participants' usage of a site or app) or ethnography (as exhibited by their behavior in their natural environment) to understand the delta between what people say they do and what they actually do.

MAKING SENSE of HUMANS:
THE ETERNAL CONUNDRUM

WhAt PEOPLE SAy thEy DO ≠ WhAt PEOPLE ActuALLy DO

READ   CAtcH up with fRiENDf   netflix

For instance, let's say you use a music streaming service for all your music needs. In a research session, if you tell me you love classical music but all I find on your playlists are Top 40 hits, I know I have more work to do to understand how you truly use the platform—and why you feel compelled to cover up your taste in music. Maybe you don't listen to classical music at all but think you should (*It sounds fancy to say I listen to classical music, doesn't it?*). Maybe you are embarrassed by your love of pop music and are hoping to cover your tracks (*"Now! That's What I Call Music" volumes 1 to 20 are my favorite albums of all time, but I can't possibly admit that.*). Or maybe you *do* like classical music but don't listen to it nearly as much as you think you do (*Has it really been that long since I listened to Vivaldi's* Four Seasons? *That used to be one of my favorites.*).

There are many reasons for why what we say may not be entirely accurate. We may feel shame when our lived experience is at odds with cultural expectations and societal norms (*Women aren't supposed to be ambitious, so I can't let them know that I am.*). We may be embarrassed by our behavior (*I'll sound like a couch potato if I admit how many hours of TV I really watch a day.*). We may resist our realities and self-protect with dishonesty (*If I don't admit it, it can't possibly be true.*).

Other times, we think we are being precise but are actually not. In fact, it can be quite hard for us to accurately estimate time intervals, forecast the future, recall the past, or even articulate our satisfaction.[1] For instance, we may underestimate how much time we've spent on a problem, or how long a problem will take us to solve. Or we say we'll be on time, that it won't take us long to get somewhere, or that it's no problem to meet a deadline, when we've actually overestimated our capabilities.

There are still other times when our estimates are nearly accurate, but easy to misinterpret. Someone who says it's hot out and lives in the deserts of Palm Springs may mean something very different from someone who says the same thing on a seventy-degree day in San Francisco. This makes for two possible axes of misinterpretation and mishap—one by the speaker, the other by the listener.

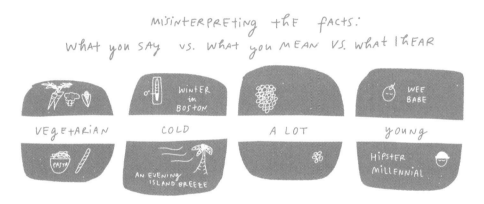

The key to effective empathetic listening is to always counterbalance what people *say* with what they *do*. Observing *actual* behaviors in addition to *stated* behaviors can help us understand people's self-perceptions, desires, and real-world routines and habits. It can also help us calibrate our own interpretation of the facts with theirs, since even when we *are* being forthright, opportunities for misinterpretation abound.

Without observation, we miss the full picture. In a research lab, that means walking away with bad data; in the real world, it can mean relating on false premises (*I love classical music, too!*) or missing a chance to relate at all (*Too bad—I actually really love Top 40.*).

Look Out for Emotion Indicators

When our aim is to connect in conversation, we will make the most progress if we focus our powers of observation on understanding emotions. If we can decode how our conversation partner is *feeling* relative to what they are saying (or leaving unsaid), we can go beyond others' polite facades, guarded nature, or edited version of themselves to get to know the real them. In addition, when we can perceive what's happening emotionally for our conversation partner in real time, we can better meet them where they are. We can walk them back from an argument to uncover what's really bothering them, or punt on having that intense discussion entirely and give them the necessary space to reset. The more we know about what they are feeling, the better we can understand them, the more appropriately we can adapt our response, and the closer we become.

To gain insight into how our conversation partner feels in the moment, there are three important elements to observe while listening: *body language* (nonverbal, gestural cues), *word choice* (the language we use), and *voice and tone* (tenor, pitch, cadence). Since each of these cues gives us information about what is happening for the other person at an emotional level, I call these *emotion indicators*. Learning to read these cues builds our emotional intelligence and our capacity to listen and respond with empathy.

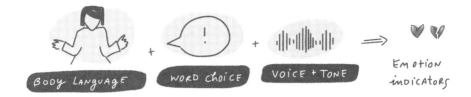

BODY LANGUAGE + WORD CHOICE + VOICE + TONE ⟹ Emotion indicators

As you learn how body language, word choice, and voice and tone cues manifest in conversation, keep in mind that though we can determine what these cues *usually* mean, they should be interpreted not in isolation but in context. A stutter, for instance, might indicate nervousness for one person, or a speech impediment for another. Use what you know of your conversation partner given your personal history and the situation to best interpret these common nonverbal cues and complement your understanding.

vs.

isolated information   contextual understanding

Body Language

My work as a researcher begins the minute you sit down. Sink back in your chair without removing your coat, clasp your hands and scoot back from the table, and I know I will need to work hard to warm you up and build rapport so you don't feel like a lab specimen, or like this is a test, for the next sixty minutes. On the other hand, if you settle in easily, taking up space at our shared desk as you spread out your accessories—bag here, jacket there, phone and water bottle in that corner—adjusting your seat back to just the right angle, accepting the snacks that we offer all participants, and that most do not accept, I can intuit that eliciting feedback from you will not take much prodding. If anything, I may have to reel you in if you begin to dominate the conversation—as you are already dominating the room. We can learn a lot about each other before a word has even been said.

Paying attention to your conversation partner's body language can give you valuable insight into what they are thinking and feeling—insight you might not otherwise gain by simply listening to their words, or that they may not be willing to verbalize at all. In particular, eye contact, how others position their hands and feet, mirroring, physical proximity, and posture can tell us much about how our partner is feeling—about a topic, environment, or present company, including you. These gestures can help us understand when rapport exists among parties, and when it is missing. They can even reveal which subjects cause our conversation partner discomfort and which are not cause for concern. More generally, they can act as a barometer for letting us know when others are at ease and when they are not. Of course, deciphering nonverbal gestures is not a one-and-done—we need to continuously track others' behavior to make meaning of it.

I like to look at four zones, each with their individual signifiers, to help interpret my conversation partner's meaning:

- Window into the soul zone

- Self-regulating zone

- Alliance zone

- Engagement zone

We'll look at how to make sense of each zone in conversation next.

WINDOW INTO THE SOUL ZONE (EYES)

Our facial expressions hold a lot of meaning. Some of us are masters of the poker face and give as little emotion away as possible. Others are an open book, easy to read whether we mean to be or not. Besides the obvious facial expressions of emotion, such as smiling, frowning, and crying, we can learn a lot about what our conversation partner is feeling simply by looking at each other eye to eye.

Eye contact—you either love it or you hate it. While everyone has personal limits for how long or intensely they can hold eye contact, its very presence is revealing.[2] Eye contact represents curiosity and openness, or even affection (think about the phrase a "lover's gaze" and you will know what I mean), and signals that you and I are both engaged in the conversation at hand. Studies show that eye contact even activates parts of the brain needed to process others' feelings and intentions—in other words, it helps us to be more empathetic.[3]

On the flip side, a lack of eye contact can signal a lack of trust or safety. If a colleague is sitting next to you, avoiding eye contact like the plague, take note. Whether the topic itself or present company has disturbed him, he seems to be uncomfortable. Though it's natural to break eye contact from time to time, and may even be beneficial when having difficult conversations, complete avoidance should be a clue that there is more work to be done to connect with your conversation partner.

SELF-REGULATING ZONE (HANDS, NECK, COLLARBONE)

Sometimes our conversation partner is more anxious than they let on. They may be all smiles, but here, our hands can be most telling. Some people click their pens, others grab a stress ball, still others bite their nails or twirl their hair. Or, they may instinctively reach for the neck or collarbone and tug at a shirt collar, play with a necklace, or simply touch the nape of their neck. When hands are busy, pay attention: This may be a sign that our conversation partner is tense or uncomfortable and attempting to calm themselves down. Their seemingly absentminded fidgeting may mean something more is on their mind.

Of course, it's possible that these gestures reflect nothing more than a tic or habit. To appropriately interpret these indicators, notice whether they surface in any predictable pattern: while discussing a specific topic (like performance reviews or other commonly stressful subjects), in certain scenarios (such as job interviews), or even in the company of a particular set of people (like in-laws). If you see signs of self-regulating, you may want to walk your conversation partner off the ledge of anxiety rather than simply pressing forward. That doesn't mean you have to call them out on their nervousness (*Are you nervous? Don't be!*)—that might only make them more nervous, especially if they are trying to keep it together with a smile. Instead, you might bring some levity to an intimidating topic, offer a break to help a nervous candidate compose themselves, or give your partner's hand a squeeze to let them know they're doing great.

ENGAGEMENT ZONE (FEET)

Sometimes it is obvious that we are losing others in conversation: if our conversation partner's eyes glaze over in boredom or they begin to bury themselves in their phone, we know they are disengaged. But often, these reactions are much more subtle. As speakers, we may not realize we are getting too technical on a topic at work, or carried away in conversation at a dinner party, or even asking too many questions at a networking event, and slowly driving our conversation partner away. What signal did we miss? Sometimes we need to look down to learn what our conversation partner really thinks.

According to Joe Navarro, former FBI agent and expert in nonverbal communication, our feet are the "most honest" part of the body and tell the strongest story about a person's true intentions.[4]

If our conversation partner's feet are pointed toward the exit, even if they are amicably chatting with us, this may indicate that they'd truthfully prefer to make an escape. They may want to jet from your conversation but are being polite, or stay behind even though they are late to a meeting out of a sense of duty or obligation. Or perhaps they are the type that has a hard time saying "no" or "I disagree"—it may be easier for them to nod and smile than admit that they aren't interested or don't agree with your advice, approach, or point of view. This kind of signaling can be quite subtle, with one foot progressively turning toward the exit and the other inching in that direction. Or, it may be obvious: if you've stopped to say hello to someone and they turn their torso toward you but keep their feet planted forward, it may not be the right time to chat. On the other hand, if their feet are pointed toward you, this may indicate they are receptive to a conversation. We naturally orient ourselves toward what we are excited by and interested in, and away from that which we are not.

When you are in search of understanding how engaged others are, take care to observe your conversation partner's footwork. How does what they are communicating with their body align with—or differ from—what they are saying? Especially when these are at odds, you will know there is more to unpack.

ALLIANCE ZONE (HIPS, TORSO, AND MIRRORING)

Some nonverbal gestures can tell us whether comfort, rapport, or even respect exist among conversation partners. Here, we can look at others' hips, torso, and mirroring, among other cues, to understand what they are feeling.

Mirroring

Mirroring is a natural subconscious process in which humans "mirror," or mimic, each other's body language. Mirroring can look like anything from smiling back at a new hire in response to their eager smile during onboarding, clapping your hands in applause in a crowded theater when others in the audience do so, picking up the gestures and mannerisms of those you spend a lot of time with, or even sitting in a similar position as your co-workers during a productive meeting. Mirroring tells us when rapport exists among the group.

When it comes to conversations, watch to see if others are naturally engaging in mirroring—this will give you a sense of when rapport exists and when it may be missing. Natural mirroring is subtle—most of us do not notice it as it happens. On the other hand, if you observe someone actively tracking your body language, quickly adjusting their posture to match yours, and forcing themselves to mimic every movement like a game of Simon Says, you may be on to a faker. Or, if your conversation partner is completely still, this may be a clue that they are uncomfortable. When rapport is lacking or even missing entirely, you may need to work harder to connect in conversation, or find a path into what you wish to talk about.

Physical Proximity

By observing how close or far individuals position themselves to each other, we can learn at a glance their comfort with one another. Sometimes this is obvious: they may deliberately choose to sit next to each other at a meeting if rapport exists, or pick seats on opposite ends of the table if the relationship is tenuous. But often it is subtle, even subconscious—here, paying close attention to the alliance zone of hips and torso can be most telling. Those who actively enjoy each other's company might lean in, pitching their torsos toward their companion if seated, or inching toward them if standing. Note that this isn't necessarily about physical affection (although it can be).

Knowing whether someone is comfortable with us or others in a group can inform our approach in conversation. For example, if I notice two teammates stiffly sitting beside each other, limbs contained as if to stay out of each other's personal space, slightly inching away from the other, I know that when it comes time to discuss pairing them on a project, I will need to broach the topic carefully and make space for a possible negative response. Or, if my own conversation partner begins to lean back as I tell a story, I can intuit that they may be running out of steam, and I'd better wrap things up.

REMEMBER THE BIG PICTURE (POSTURE)

Decoding zones one by one will take us far, but to make the most of our powers of observation, we need to put all the pieces together. Posture—the way someone carries themselves from head to toe—can reveal the big picture of what our conversation partner thinks, feels, or means. When we can't see our conversation partner in full, we are likely to understand only part of the story. That's why, if you've ever tried to "read" someone over a video call where you could see only their face, you may have found it extra challenging.

An easy way to interpret someone's posture is to look at how much space they take up in a room. Physical size has little to do with it—even the tiniest teammate can seem large by stretching her legs out and propping them up on a table in front of her, elbows bent to the side, and hands interlaced behind her head. She is signaling with her posture that she is comfortable and in control. On the other hand, even a tall person can seem small if they hunch their shoulders, cross their legs, and fold their arms tightly over their chest. These may be habits acquired long ago, or signal a lack of confidence—in themselves or in their ideas—or even a wish to avoid confrontation.

Our conversation partner's posture relative to others in a group can also be revealing. For example, in a room full of seated colleagues, if a single person remains standing, you can bet they hold some power. The same dynamic can surface in settings as casual as a dinner party—the host who stays standing as guests settle into their seats appears at ease and in charge in their role. People who take up space in these ways may be expressing confidence, certainty, control, seriousness, or even asserting dominance.

Noticing this proves fruitful in conversation. If we need to facilitate a team discussion or conversation among friends, understanding the group's dynamics can help us to moderate it more effectively and ensure that even those who are backing away in their seat have a voice in the conversation. If we need buy-in from a group to make a decision, we may want to partner with our more dominant friend or colleague to influence others. If we notice our conversation partners consistently make themselves small in our presence, we know we may have to work twice as hard to create a safe space within which to engage them.

Consider these nonverbal gestures and their common meanings below the next time you are in conversation. As you do, remember that reading body language is more art than science. Incorporate what you know of your conversation partner and a given situation to make the most sense of what you are hearing—and seeing.

NONVERBAL GESTURES AND THEIR COMMON MEANINGS

Zone	Gesture	Emotion
Window into the Soul	Eye contact	Connection, confidence, focus
	Smiling	Happy, cooperative, polite
	Frowning	Sadness, confusion, worry
Self-Regulating	Neck touching	Insecurity, distress, discomfort
	Hand on collarbone	Concern, shock, stress
	Nail biting	Boredom, unease, anxiety
	Clenched fists	Frustration, anger, restraint
	Fidgety fingers, hand-wringing	Nervousness, distress, worry
Engagement	Feet pointed away	Ready to leave, disinterested
	Feet pointed toward	Committed, interested
Alliance	Leaning toward	Comfort, agreement
	Crossed arms	Defensiveness, insecurity
	Open arms	Receptive, eager, warm
	"Large" postures (outstretched arms and legs)	Territorial, dominance
	"Small" postures (crossed arms and legs, hunched shoulders)	Unease, lack of confidence

Word Choice

The first time my manager Henry gave me feedback, I was excited. (Nerd alert.) At the time, I was a researcher at a midsize tech company. I'd been there for over a year and worked on a variety of projects, but I had only been reporting to Henry for about six months; in classic growing start-up fashion, he was my third manager in less than a year. As a firm believer that feedback, with the right intent, can help you grow and develop, I was looking forward to learning how I could improve.

To start, Henry outlined my strengths, drawn from conversations with my cross-functional team, the people I collaborated with day-to-day, who were stakeholders in my studies and consumers of my insights. The product managers I worked with appreciated my thoughtful prioritization of high-impact work. The designers felt they had a strong partner and collaborator who pushed their design thinking forward. The engineers better understood who they were building for, thanks to my efforts. In general, my day-to-day teams were happy.

"Your cross-functionals love you," Henry said. "But on the research team—the feedback is a little soft."

Henry stopped there, and his words hung in the air. Soft? What did that mean? Were we talking about the whole team (I hoped not!), or a specific person? I was concerned to hear that there was negative feedback coming from this group, since the research team was my "home" team. If cross-functionals were more akin to friends, the research team was more like family—the people I saw every day and whose function I shared—and I didn't want to let them down. I asked Henry for more clarity, and he said, "Well, the feeling is just a little squishy coming from the research side." I had no idea what that meant.

Eventually, after a lot of back-and-forth, I learned that a teammate had given critical feedback on my approach to a specific project: "A little too aggressive," Henry finally relayed, but once more he stopped short of providing specifics. On the one hand, I was relieved to hear more, because I felt like it gave me something to work on. On the other, the feedback remained vague and inactionable. I pressed for more detail. As Henry went on, I was like a machete-wielding explorer lost in the jungle. I had to cut through a lot of vague phrases to gain an understanding of what the feedback actually meant and how I could grow from it.

The words people use tell us a lot about their beliefs, opinions, emotions, and even their values. In this instance, I learned a few things about my new manager. First, he was very uncomfortable with giving critical feedback. Second, both to ease his discomfort and to prevent hurting my feelings, he had attempted to keep his feedback as vague as possible. Third, despite his lack of specificity, he believed the feedback was valuable—that there was something there for me to work on.

If I had focused on the content of Henry's words alone, I would have walked away from our feedback session stumped. Untangling his word choice allowed me to understand not only his feedback, but also *him* better. In future performance conversations with Henry, I made sure to ask for specificity to help make the feedback actionable, and to encourage him to keep the feedback coming, even if it was critical.

You can make sense of word choice by looking at the following commonly used phrases, which usually indicate your conversation partner has more to say.

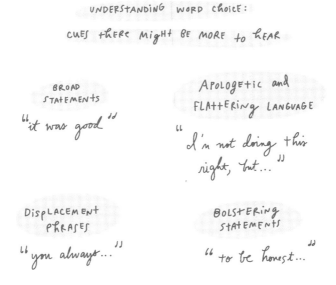

UNDERSTANDING WORD CHOICE:
CUES THERE MIGHT BE MORE TO HEAR

BROAD
STATEMENTS
"it was good"

APOLOGETIC and
FLATTERING LANGUAGE
"I'm not doing this
right, but..."

DisPLACEMENT
PHRASES
"you always..."

BOLSTERING
STATEMENTS
"to be honest..."

BROAD STATEMENTS

Phrases like "I like it," "it's good," "sure," and "whatever" are often signals that there is more to be said. They are usually employed when people are afraid of offering their honest opinion for fear of appearing controversial, hurting someone's feelings, or not being appropriately invested in the topic at hand. When you hear broad statements like these, you can gently follow up to get more clarity, remembering that your conversation partner's choice of words already speaks volumes.

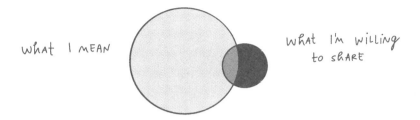

Depending on the relationship, it may be more productive to carefully coax out your conversation partner's honest opinion, or to call them out directly to be more specific. Choose accordingly and say something like:

- Help me understand what you mean by . . .
- What do you [like, dislike] about . . . ?
- Tell me how you really feel.

APOLOGETIC AND FLATTERING LANGUAGE

In the research lab, we often present participants with prototypes, or partially functional versions of our product, sometimes filled with deliberately out-there ideas. We might experiment with changes like removing the home screen (where users land by default in an app), changing the visual design (what things look like), or even eliminating an important button users have become accustomed to (like an archive button in an email inbox). We call these "concepts" and "ideas" when talking to participants, but among researchers we refer to the most outlandish ideas as "provocations"—we are deliberately trying something wild to get a reaction.

We expect many of these provocations to fail miserably when

put in front of users, and many rightfully do. But even when sharing the worst of the worst ideas, we inevitably hear apologetic language from participants, who feel obliged to soften the blow that what we've created is totally useless. "I bet this feature would be great for a lot of people—I'm probably just not using this right," they say. "I'm sure the way I listen to music isn't complicated enough for these kinds of advanced settings, but for most people it would probably be great!"

Like broad statements, apologetic and flattering language can be a signal of discomfort, and a reflection of our very human desire to please others. Out of fear of disappointing or offending, we may hide behind "It must be me" thinking and "This is beyond my understanding" rationalizations.

If you find yourself on the receiving end of apologetic and flattering language, reinforce to your conversation partner why their real and complete perspective is valuable to you. For example, in research, because I know many people harbor a tendency to please, I will do everything in my power to encourage their honest response. If they tell me, "I'm not sure this would work for me personally, but I can see this being so helpful for most people," I stress the importance of *their* opinion above all by saying something like, "I'm so interested in the way *you* use the platform. Tell me more about *that*!" When that interest is genuine, they are more likely to open up, and eventually share exactly how the idea falls short.

Without follow-ups like these, we may never really know what our conversation partner thinks. The phrases below can help you reach the heart of the matter when apologetic and flattering language is getting in the way:

- I value your perspective on this. Please don't hold back.

- Your honest opinion means a lot to me. What else comes to mind?

- I always learn so much from your ideas. I'd love to hear more.

- Your input is invaluable. Tell me how this is landing.

STALLING

Stalling, or the act of speaking in vague terms to slow or even derail a conversation for our own purposes, typically occurs when we want to buy ourselves time to come up with a response, formulate an idea, or delay a decision. It usually arises in response to a question or idea posed by our conversation partner. We tend to rely on this technique when we believe the truth is insufficient—either because we fear it makes us look bad, is not polite or sufficiently kind, or even adequately thorough—and are not comfortable being honest with others as a result.

For example, if I ask a participant for their assessment of a potential product and say, "What are your thoughts on this product?" and they respond, "What are my thoughts on this product?," no matter what they tell me next, I can bet their real answer is not positive. In repeating my question back to me, they are buying themselves time—to make sense of their true feelings, to craft a polite response, or even to comprehend the question itself. If the answer were obvious, and positive (*I love it!*), they would likely not need time to gather their thoughts or choose their words so carefully. We often go with our gut when we are confident in our response and comfortable sharing it, and find ways to stall when we are not.

Stalling comes up in everyday conversation, too. In a job interview, a candidate may rely on stalling to buy time to answer a difficult question, or even spin a lie (*I can't tell them I was let go at my last job, so let me see what else I can say here.*). At a lecture or conference, a presenter who is caught off guard by an audience member's question or prefers not to answer it may stall in order to subtly divert the question and avoid embarrassment (*This question is out of my wheelhouse, but I want to look credible, so I need to find a way to change the subject to one I can speak to.*). This technique can also surface when we want to protect ourselves or others from a difficult situation (*I can't admit I forgot our anniversary or we'll wind up arguing. How can I quickly cover this up?*).

Whether stalling is used to self-protect or protect others, it is a mark of hesitation, and tells us our conversation partner may be holding back.

Signs of stalling may include:

- **Affirming.** Acknowledging what's been said in lieu of directly responding to it. Affirming sounds like: "That's a great question." "That's an interesting observation."

- **Parroting.** Asking the same question, verbatim, that was originally posed to them—as the participant did with me. You'll notice when it happens because it sounds so unnatural.

- **Deflecting.** Responding to a different question than was asked. It is a classic political debate move: "I'm glad you asked about education policy in America. When I was a little girl, . . ."

If a stalling or bolstering phrase crosses your path, take note. Depending on the relationship, your approach may vary.

When trust exists between you and your conversation partner, you may want to encourage your conversation partner to be more forthcoming. Try the following phrases:

- I'm sensing some [hesitation, avoidance, uncertainty, etc.]. Be honest with me about how you are feeling.

- It seems like we are dancing around this topic. How do you really feel about it?

- It feels as if there may be more to be said on this one. Tell me about your current thinking.

- I sense you may be holding back. What's really on your mind?

For less intimate relationships, this type of encouragement can sound invasive, or even accusatory. Instead, you can gently give your conversation partner the space to find their words. Here, offering a warm smile and a bit of patience can help them share more on their own terms. We can all empathize with feeling rushed, nervous, confused, or protective about what we want to say next.

Other times, you may find it to your advantage to say nothing in the moment and instead observe and learn from others' behavior for the future. For instance, if stalling is consistent, this may be a sign of a lack of trust in your relationship, or an indication that others are not comfortable sharing how they feel with you—it may be more productive to build this relationship over time than to address it in real time.

BOLSTERING STATEMENTS

No matter how much or for how long we withhold our feelings, there comes a time where we are finally ready to share more. Phrases such as "To be honest," "To tell you the truth," "If I'm being candid," and "For transparency" are often used to admit how we feel. They may also be used to emphasize or reinforce our position and ensure that we are not misunderstood. If we held back out of fear, we may now have the courage to move forward (*This feedback will be difficult to give, but I have to stand up for myself.*). If our desire to be patient or polite kept us from being transparent, we may now need to move things along and share our true feelings (*I've given him the floor for some time, but it's time for me to respectfully disagree with his approach.*). When intentions are good, such phrases are usually used sparingly, which is part of what makes them so effective.

But these same phrases, used in excess, may be a sign that someone is trying hard to convince you they are being honest, but are actually not. They are what Pamela Meyer, author of *Liespotting*, calls "bolstering statements."[5] They may be employed when others withhold the truth to protect themselves (*I can't admit that I don't have the right skill set for the job, so I'll just bluff my way through it.*), build alliances with others (*I'll just tell her what she wants to hear, and she'll agree to my idea.*), avoid hurting other people's feelings (*It's easier to tell him everything is great than to admit I'm unhappy in this relationship.*), or even because honesty wasn't modeled for them growing up (*Lying is just how this is done.*). It's worth pausing when you hear these phrases in excess to consider whether you're getting the whole truth, or whether there's more to be said.

When you hear a bolstering statement, be sure to incorporate other cues—such as body language, voice and tone, and even what you know about this particular individual—to help you decipher whether their use of these phrases is little more than a verbal tic, a sign that your conversation partner has steeled up their courage or wishes to emphasize their feelings, or whether they might actually be deliberately concealing something from you.

DISPLACEMENT PHRASES

Ever had a roommate you didn't get along with? Maybe you hated how they left the dishes in the sink for days on end. "You always leave a mess in the kitchen," you might say when your roommate rage boiled over. "Well you never take the trash out," they might gripe in return.

OK, so maybe this isn't a roommate match made in heaven—but are these kinds of arguments really just about chores?

Phrases such as "You say," "You always," and "You never" are worth paying attention to. I call these *displacement phrases* because they are often used to displace a feeling we have about ourselves with a feeling we have about someone else. Often, this blame masks a deeper emotion that needs our attention. Anger, disappointment, loneliness, and fear can be uncomfortable to sit in; displacing them onto others gives us a way out. Because it is far easier to focus on how others are at fault than to interrogate what we are feeling and where it is coming from, displacement phrases come up more often than we'd like to admit, and especially in close relationships—whether with roommates, family, or even spouses.

In the case of our bickering roommates, who does the dishes or takes out the trash is just the beginning. Often, such arguments belie deeper discontent: we may be feeling unappreciated and ignored, disrespected and taken advantage of, or simply low after a difficult day at work. Soon the fighting gloves are on, and displacement phrases abound.

Although it's easy to want to ignore, argue, or reject displacement phrases when you hear them, they are a chance to learn more about our conversation partner and the deeper emotions they may be harboring. Let them fester too long, and you may find yourself with a broken friendship and in search of a new roommate.

In the presence of displacement phrases, try these responses to keep the conversation going and dig deeper into the underlying emotion. Remember to tread carefully, since the closer you get to the underlying emotion, the more tender it may be.

- I'm wondering if we are still talking about [the dirty dishes, the unmet deadline, who paid the bill last, etc.]. Is there something more going on?

- I'm noticing our conversation is escalating; is . . . still the problem, or is this about something else?

- I think I may have upset you, but I'm not sure if it's about . . . anymore.

- I can see talking about this is important to you; help me understand your reaction.

Voice and Tone

Like many of us, I get a lump in my throat when I'm about to cry, and my voice starts to tremble and slightly crack. I can feel it when it's about to happen, and if they're paying attention, my conversation partner can pick up on it, too. I'm not embarrassed by this response, but I'm certainly not in control of it: my voice is revealing something about my emotions whether I want it to or not.

In the same way, *pacing* (how quickly or slowly one speaks), *pitch* (how high or low one's voice is), and *volume* (how softly or loudly one projects) can tell us much about what our conversation partner means and how they are feeling.

A colleague raising her voice more loudly than usual may be signaling her frustration, and a partner talking a mile a minute may be exhibiting urgency in getting his feelings out. The wavering of a friend's voice lets us know they are upset, and the brightness of a smile can be heard over the phone, even if you can't see your conversation partner. You can even glean much from the sound of a hum, in the absence of any words at all. From joy to sadness, our emotions commonly manifest through voice and tone.

DECODING THE SOUNDS OF OUR EMOTIONS

Positive Emotions (Joy, Enthusiasm, Calm)	Negative Emotions (Fear, Sadness, Anger, Disgust)
Bright	Somber
Musical	Dissonant
Smooth, even	Wavering, halting

EXERCISE: Hum Through It

Test your skills in decoding voice cues with this simple exercise: Ask a friend to hum through a conversation to see what meaning you can glean. In the absence of words, worry less about the details you may be missing and aim to understand emotions instead. What can you learn from a simple hum?

PACING

My colleague Nel is the type of person who labors carefully over every word she says. Conversations with her cannot be rushed: she is deliberately choosing her words as she goes, processing ideas in real time. Our one-on-ones tend to go over, in part because this approach is so time-consuming. Though I was at first thrown by this method, I have since become accustomed to it and understand it is a reflection of her learning and communication style. But on occasion, Nel surprises me. Her cadence speeds way up. Rather than pause for the perfect phrase, she unloads a rapid-fire set of sentences, speaking in long paragraphs. In these moments, relative to her normal verbal style, she says a lot more in a much shorter amount of time.

A change of pace can be indicative of a number of emotions. Suddenly slowing down can reveal a need to deliberate or think things through, or can reflect stability and control. You may have experienced this yourself if you have ever stopped to carefully choose your words during a difficult conversation. Too dramatic a slowdown in speech, however, and this can indicate annoyance, or even condescension.

On the other hand, our conversation partner may speed up their speech when they are nervous, as many job candidates do when presenting their portfolio to a room full of strangers. A fast-paced conversation may also be a sign of excitement—when others are bursting with ideas, they may be quick with enthusiasm to verbalize them. Pay close attention to rapid-fire speech in particular when it comes from those who are otherwise slow and steady in their delivery. This kind of deviation from the norm is worth tuning in to, for it tells us that this moment is different from others.

After a few conversations with Nel, I noticed that her normally deliberate pace quickens most often after receiving critical feedback, when she is upset and feels overwhelmed by the situation at hand. Learning this about her has helped me participate in our conversations in a different way: it has led me to slow down and relate to her on an emotional level rather than a rational one, because that's what her voice is telling me she needs. Approaching conversations in this way ensures I don't overwhelm Nel, so that she can leave our meeting ready to take charge instead of ready to run away.

PITCH

Our voices have a natural range in which we speak, and, as with pacing, deviations from the norm can indicate a change in emotion. In a research session, when a participant who starts off animated suddenly becomes monotone, I know something—the topic, their energy level, me—has turned them off in some way. When this happens, I may decide to slow down my question-asking, or hit pause on a topic and revisit it in a different way later in order to keep the conversation going. In the real world, these same changes in pitch can be revealing: they tell us whether a first date is going well or is simply boring, whether someone is the bearer of good news or bad, or whether someone is happy to see us or merely tolerant of our presence.

In addition to emotions, our pitch can also reveal something about our intentions. For instance, mothers instinctively speak in a higher register to soothe or calm their newborns. In a similar way, an employee gearing up for an important conversation may intentionally lower her pitch to project an image of authority and power. We may even subconsciously change our pitch when we are in the presence of someone we believe to be powerful, employing a submissive, higher-pitched voice around them.[6]

The following common cues can help you gain insight into what your conversation partner is feeling.

PAY ATTENTION TO PITCH	
Pitch	**Meaning**
Low	Authoritative, dominant
High	Unserious, submissive
Squeaky, whiny	Unstable, childish, insecure
Sharp	Commanding, tense
Expressive	Engaged, enthusiastic
Monotone	Disengaged, bored

When you observe a change in pitch from your conversation partner, do your best to understand what might be driving it. Listen closely for a few minutes before reading too much into things. By giving your conversation partner time to return their pitch to normal, you will hear more clearly what causes a change in pitch, and when variation is mere coincidence.

VOLUME

Though there are physical factors that affect our natural volume in conversation, much of how loudly or quietly we speak is a reflection of how we feel about ourselves, others, or even a topic of conversation. For instance, shyness, lack of concentration, nervousness, and self-consciousness are all associated with speaking softly. Your conversation partner may wish to blend in and not draw attention to themselves, or have run out of steam on a tough problem and be too low-energy to speak at a normal volume. On the other hand, a conversation partner who speaks louder than normal may exude confidence, dominance, and even aggression. They may raise their voice out of a need to make their point be heard, to rise to the challenge at hand, or because they feel pressured to defend their territory in conversation.

In a research session, even if I have only just met a participant, their normal range reveals itself in a matter of minutes. Even more telling is when I hear a change in volume—then I know to listen up. Sometimes it is a topic that makes someone uncomfortable. Other times, and especially in groups, it is a sign that their comfort sharing with the group has changed—they may feel more or less safe to contribute, depending on the group's dynamics and how the session is going. A shift in volume is my clue to decode what someone is feeling, and why.

When voice volume is dialed up or down, pay attention to what came before and after this change. Have you hit a sensitive spot and inadvertently caused your conversation partner to raise their voice in self-protection? Has an otherwise confident-sounding job candidate suddenly become soft-spoken, perhaps a reflection of their discomfort, when it came time for their salary negotiation? Has a member of the group grown quiet in discussion in response to a peer's continuous rejection of his ideas? Even if you do not know your conversation partner well, you can track a change in volume throughout the course of your discussion, and begin to identify what emotions might be causing those changes.

EXERCISE: **Train Your Ear**

In your next conversation, see what you can learn about others by paying attention to their speaking patterns. What does their "neutral" or typical voice sound like? Track the following attributes to gain insight into their present experience:

- **Pitch:** How high or low is their voice?
- **Pacing:** How quickly or slowly do they speak?
- **Volume:** Do they naturally project, or are they soft-spoken?
- **Expressiveness:** Is their speech dynamic and animated or monotone?
- **Rhythm:** What is the natural rhythm of their speech?
- **Tone:** What is the general character of how they speak?

Once you have identified "normal" for a given conversation partner, listen for any changes as you chat and pay close attention to when these occur.

- How do each of the aforementioned attributes change in a given moment?
- What does a departure from normalcy sound like?
- What emotions might be driving those changes?
- In whose company do these changes occur?
- On what subjects are these changes apparent?
- What might these changes signal overall?

BEFORE YOU FORGET

Body language, word choice, and voice quality offer us a fuller, more nuanced understanding of what our conversation partner is experiencing. Through careful observation, try to understand what these cues indicate about you, the conversation topic, and the surrounding environment and deepen the conversation.

Part II

NAVIGATE THE CONVERSATION

CHAPTER 4

Clarify Your Role

I was at my local breakfast spot when a woman walked in. "I am so frustrated with my sister," she said, sliding into a booth with three of her friends. "She completely missed my daughter's birthday. Her own niece. Her only niece!"

"Such a bummer!" one friend said. "So self-centered," another added.

"I really wanted it to be a special day," the woman said. "Having to make excuses for why her aunt hadn't called was tough. I could understand if my sister had more nieces and nephews to keep track of, but she only has one."

The third friend had observed from behind her plate of pancakes and piped in. "Could it be that she forgot, but didn't mean anything by it? Didn't she have that big deadline coming up at work, the one with . . . ?" She stopped as the group looked back, their eyes wide, as if to say *Hello! What is wrong with you?*

Each of us has a natural way of stepping into conversation: an instinctive mode we tune in to without thinking. You may be a problem-solver by nature, ready to help a friend or colleague troubleshoot whatever is on their mind. Or perhaps you are more the cheerleading type, often complimentary, knowing just how to inspire your direct report to keep going on that challenging project they've taken on. Maybe you are like the friend at my breakfast spot, always trying to consider things from others' points of view, even when it might not be welcome. There are many ways to show up in a conversation, but we tend to play one role more often than the rest.

I call this our *default listening mode.* It is influenced by our unique temperament, how we've been socialized, and even cultural expectations. For many of us, chances are it started to take form during childhood, in response to our early relationships and the environment around us, and has been reinforced time and again since then and throughout our lives.

Sometimes our default mode is exactly what's called for in conversation, but sometimes it's not. Whether out of respect or politeness (a relationship between a manager and a direct report), cultural expectations and norms (always speak your mind, or never speak up around elders), topic (your favorite hobby versus a subject you know little about), or need (to be coached or to be directed), certain dynamics may ask us to shift from one listening mode to another in conversation. Failure to adapt can lead to miscommunications, awkwardness, and even conflict, all of which can make it difficult to maintain a connection. A direct report who always gets advice from her manager when she is merely hoping to provide visibility on her progress may start to feel micromanaged and disrespected.

A friend playing devil's advocate instead of cheerleader may cause cracks in a friendship and have to work hard to regain trust.

That's why it's so important to align our listening expectations and habits to what our conversation partner needs at that moment. Once we do, we can move in lockstep together: We know when it's time to celebrate our direct report's progress, not point out what's still left to be done. We understand when it's more important to quietly listen as our sibling describes a stressful day, rather than come up with a plan to relieve their stress or talk about our own. We sense when our roommate needs comfort, and when it would be better to leave them alone. We intuit when a sense of humor is called for in a tense meeting, and when empathy is what's needed to keep the group together. Over time, the more successful exchanges we have, the stronger our relationships become.

To be a more effective listener, we must understand our default listening mode, uncover what our conversation partner needs from us in a given discussion, and adapt accordingly. The tips to come will show you how.

Common Default Listening Modes

As a researcher, my job is to be a neutral and objective listener. The way I show up in sessions—kind without being effusive, impartial without being detached, encouraging without biasing a response—stems from years of training, and helps me to receive, understand, and guide a participant in order to get to the bottom of whatever question we are working on. It's easy to spot a researcher clicking into "researcher mode" if you know what to look for.

Similarly, in the real world, we can learn to spot certain listening modes. Though our conversations may vary across a given topic, set of conversation partners, and our own personalities, even in an average conversation there are some modes that are more common than the rest, and identifiable if we are paying attention.

Below are the most common default listening modes, each with its own strengths and weaknesses. As you enter in conversation, listen for when these modes are surfacing, and with whom.

> **The Explainer.** Explainers have an answer for everything, especially when it comes to our feelings (*You're feeling burned out? It must be because of our culture of overworking.*). Rational thinking can provide welcome perspective and help us gain distance from our feelings. Still, Explainers must catch themselves not to go overboard, since we don't always want an explanation for our

emotions; that type of response can come across as short-sighted and dismissive.

The Validator. It can feel great to talk to a Validator, especially when you are in need of a pick-me-up (*Yeah, it is their fault! They don't understand you!*). These natural cheerleaders are always on our side, but unchecked, Validators can unintentionally inflate your ego, skew your perspective, and even stunt your personal growth.

The Identifier. Identifying happens when a listener likens their experience to the speaker's and brings a conversation back to them. "I know exactly what you mean." "I felt the same way when . . ." "It's like how when I . . ." These responses can help us to feel less alone in our experience. At the same time, not everyone craves affirmation; in these cases, identifying responses can be disconnecting. They show the listener that we aren't listening at all—we're thinking about ourselves.

The Problem-Solver. Problem-Solvers have a solution for everything and are the perfect sounding board when you need to make progress or improve an idea. The catch is when a Problem-Solver solves "problems" that don't exist. You might have simply been thinking aloud, but to a Problem-Solver in overdrive, everything you say is an opportunity to fix, solve, or rectify.

The Nurse. The Nurse puts your needs above theirs. It's never too late for them to run an errand on your behalf, or too much to tend to you when you're feeling down. But the more they take care of you, the more your relationship tips out of balance. Not only can all that care feel overwhelming, but it's also all too easy for a Nurse to focus so much on *you* that you never get to support *them*.

The Defuser. Defusers are known to play down tense or uncomfortable situations, often using jokes. When a dose of levity is called for, their humor is helpful. On the other hand, if a Defuser makes light of every situation, especially ones that are difficult for you, it may be hard to feel close to them.

The Mediator. Mediators love to look at things from all angles and assume good intent, and make great company for mitigating conflict. But like the friend at the café, in an effort to understand everyone's perspectives, they can sometimes inadvertently make it feel unsafe to share our point of view at all.

The Empath. Empaths have an uncanny way of tuning in to your emotional experience—sometimes even before you do. "I sense you are feeling weighed down lately," they may say, "Is everything OK?" It can be comforting to be seen by Empaths in this way. To be most effective, Empaths must read cues carefully and ensure there is trust in the relationship; without it, their intuitions about how we feel can unintentionally make us feel exposed and even suspicious (*How do they know so much about me?*).

The Interrupter. Interrupters are always one step ahead of us—or so they think. At their best, Interrupters make spirited conversation partners. At their worst, Interrupters can be tiring—as quickly as they jump in, it can feel like everyone else is shut out.

The Interviewer. Interviewers are known to ask their conversation partner lots of questions. Their genuine curiosity can make us feel valued. Nevertheless, asking too many questions can make conversations feel like interrogations. This approach also shields Interviewers from having to share their own stories, making it difficult to get to know them.

The Daydreamer. Daydreamers are often lost in thought during conversations. Whether due to rich imaginations or anxious minds, their tendency to distract isn't personal, but it can make us feel less than worthy of their time. "What were you saying again?" quickly becomes a tiring refrain.

These modes are helpful to be aware of. Recognizing them in *others* gives us insight into who they are; if I understand that you are a chronic problem-solver, I know not to take it personally when you give me unsolicited advice on a challenge I am working through, because that is simply your way. Recognizing these modes in *ourselves* helps us to better regulate our responses in conversation. It is much easier to catch if we are slipping into a mode that may not be welcome—and to do something about it—when we know there is a range of other modes we can tap into instead.

Self-Reflect: Identify Your Default Listening Mode

To help identify your habitual response in conversation, consider the listening modes you just learned about and answer the following questions:

- What do you think is your default listening mode?

COMMON LISTENING MODES

THE EXPLAINER — THAT'S BECAUSE...

THE VALIDATOR — YOU'RE RIGHT

THE IDENTIFIER — ME, TOO

THE PROBLEM-SOLVER — HERE'S WHAT TO DO

THE NURSE — EVERYTHING WILL BE OKAY

THE DEFUSER — HOW ABOUT A JOKE?

THE MEDIATOR — I'M SURE THEY MEANT DIFFERENTLY

THE EMPATH — THAT SOUNDS TOUGH; I'M SORRY TO HEAR IT

THE INTERRUPTER — ! — !

THE INTERVIEWER — —?—?—?

THE DAYDREAMER —

Which ONE ARE you?

- What would your friends say? How about your parents? Your co-workers?
- In what scenarios might your default mode change, if at all?

Listen for Hidden Needs

My team and I were conducting a study on how knowledge workers collaborate in remote work environments. Because we hoped to design a set of tools that would help not just individuals but teams work better together, we decided to run triads. Unlike the more traditional one-on-one interview, each session would bring together three members of a team to answer our questions.

"Tell me about how you currently collaborate at work," I asked the first group of participants.

"I'd say this is one of the strengths of our team," the team lead, Jess, told me. "We really value being able to talk through ideas together, whether by phone, in a shared doc, via email, or chat messaging."

Her manager, Yael, chimed in. "Jess has done a great job of setting our team up so we can collaborate no matter where we are."

I nodded, then turned to the third and most junior teammate, a new grad named Leah. Leah had remained fairly quiet during our session so far. Unlike Jess and Yael, she only piped in when spoken to directly.

"How about you, Leah?" I asked. "I understand your role is a bit different than Jess and Yael. What is collaboration like for you?"

"I love working with my team, and Jess's work has helped us all stay connected," Leah said. "Virtual collaboration can be overwhelming sometimes, but I'm probably just bad at managing my time. I'm learning as I go."

As I listened to Leah, I picked up on a few key details. "It's probably me" was an apologetic phrase that suggested she felt the need to take accountability: perhaps she didn't want to point out a flaw in Jess's strategy, or she assumed that if things were working for everyone else, it must be her fault. Mentioning that she was learning on the fly indicated that her routine was in flux, with room for improvement. And saying collaboration could be "sometimes overwhelming" suggested there was a range in how well things worked, and that things could occasionally get pretty bad. Though she hadn't explicitly said so, I could hear that Leah was struggling. Given these cues and the circumstances—that Leah, a junior employee, was being asked to share her candid opinion in front of her leadership team—along with an observable pattern of holding back and waiting for others to weigh in first, I intuited that there was more to dig into.

But as quickly as Leah shared her reality, Jess and Yael diagnosed her response: "That used to happen to me all the time," Jess said. "I can send you a great article on time management." "Let's chat later about what we can take off your plate," Leah's manager added.

Leah politely thanked her teammates, then quickly trained her attention back on me. She was quiet after that. But to get a full picture of how our product should support teams like hers, I needed to understand Leah's point of view more deeply. I didn't want to push her too far—and especially not in front of her co-workers—so I asked the magic wand question, a common research tool that allows participants to share their honest feedback without fear of offending others. To give Leah the space to speak up without the bias of her teammates, I directed my question to her first.

"Imagine you have a magic wand. With it, you can design your ideal work from home experience. What would that look like for you?" I asked.

Leah began to think aloud: "Back at the office, there was an unwritten code that if you were wearing headphones you were busy, and people wouldn't interrupt you. But now that we are remote, we are all 'always on'—there's no such thing as putting your headphones on. In an ideal world, I could let someone know if I'm in the zone, and would know when not to interrupt them, too."

By having the room and encouragement to express her needs, Leah was able to identify a crucial pitfall in remote work: the same tools that encourage virtual collaboration tend to distract us from deep work. She hadn't needed sympathy or even problem-solving from others—but she did need an opening to speak up. When she did, Leah shared great ideas that could help us improve our product and her workflow.

More often than not, we do not make our needs clear in a conversation, out of fear, awkwardness, vulnerability, or simply lack of self-awareness. Like Leah, our conversation partner may be their own worst critic and cast blame on themselves, minimize their needs, or hide them from others entirely. Or, they may be ready to ask for help but are uncertain how to do it, as many of us are when we are navigating a new or imbalanced relationship. They may even have ideas to share but fear rejection and need the space and encouragement to voice them. In other cases, they may not know what they need and talk around their needs before getting there—either because they are still processing what they feel or because their emotions are clouding their communication. Or perhaps they think, as many of us so often do, that they are being explicit in stating their needs, when they are actually inadvertently hiding them behind wishes, what-ifs, and if-onlys.

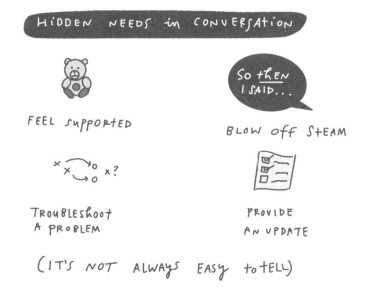

Conversations in which our partner's needs are not obvious to us make it easy to miss the mark on why we're here and where we're going. That's why before we respond with advice, suggest a solution, or otherwise take action in conversation, we have to understand what it is our conversation partner is seeking, and what our role in meeting those needs should be.

To identify what our conversation partners need from us, we need to use our informed intuition of what's happening, catch cues that reveal underlying meaning, and ask clarifying questions about how we can help.

INFORM YOUR INTUITION

You can begin to understand what your conversation partner needs from you by leaning on your *informed intuition*, a combination of what your gut is telling you plus what you know to be true about a given scenario, person, or yourself. With careful observation in the moment and self-reflection as to what you might bring to the table, you might find you know more than has been said.

To put your informed intuition together and evaluate what's needed, consider the following:

- **Your conversation partner's personal history.** Start with what you know about your partner. Ask yourself: Does this person typically come to me for advice? Want a hug when they are down? Tend to minimize their emotions and quickly move on?

- **The current situation.** Observe verbal and nonverbal cues like body language, word choice, and voice quality to determine what your conversation partner may be feeling at that moment. Consider: Is this scenario exciting or scary? Risky or safe? Urgent or trivial? Do I have sufficient context?

- **Your unique qualities and characteristics.** What attributes do you possess that make you uniquely suited to meet their needs, if any? Though you may not have identified your conversation partner's needs yet, you can begin to explore why they might have chosen to share their thoughts with you in particular. What might you be bringing out in them? Think: Do I have the expertise they need? What can I offer here?

For instance, in my session with Leah, I had a lot of information to work with, such as her reticence, body language, and her role within the team, along with the experience to know that the lab setting can make participants uncomfortable, especially when power dynamics are in play. From her teammates' behavior, I sensed that they were much more at ease than Leah and might have even mistakenly assumed she felt the same way. This helped me intuit that Leah might need more space and encouragement to share how she really felt.

ASK YOURSELF: WHAT'S NEEDED IN THIS MOMENT?

AM I BEING ASKED TO PROBLEM-SOLVE?

AM I BEING ASKED TO VALIDATE?

AM I BEING ASKED FOR COMPANY?

CATCH CUES

Sometimes you will have a strong intuition about how best to adapt your listening mode in the moment, as I did with Leah. For instance, if a friend sobs about how unhappy she is at work, you may conclude that now is not the time to problem-solve and suggest she start looking for other jobs: that could be considered insensitive, and besides, she's likely already thought of that.

But sometimes, our instinct is fuzzier. When the signs are uncertain, we'll want to listen for cues to help us uncover our conversation partner's underlying needs and pivot our listening mode accordingly. Keep your ears tuned to the following signs that a need is emerging. (See the table on the next page.) If you hear these often subtle phrases, stop and consider what might be driving them.

LISTEN FOR HIDDEN NEEDS

Cue	Meaning
• I wish that . . . • If only I could . . . • If I had things my way . . . • If it were up to me, I'd . . . • In an ideal world . . .	Desire, opportunity, lack, shortcoming
• I'm swamped • I'm exhausted • I'm running out of steam • I haven't gotten as much done as I would have liked to today	Plea for help
• I miss . . . • I've been thinking about when . . . • It's been a while since . . .	Nostalgia
• I'm working as hard as I can • I'm going out of my way here • I'm doing the best I can	Plea for recognition
• I never know what to do when . . . • I can't figure out . . . • I'm at a loss . . .	Need for direction

ASK THEM TO SPELL IT OUT

If you can tell that your default listening mode is not the right match for your conversation partner—because they react poorly, or tell you point-blank that what you're saying isn't helpful—but the path forward is unclear, it may be time to ask them to spell it out. Here, *clarifying questions*—questions that explicitly ask our conversation partner for direction on how best to respond—show us the way forward. I recommend asking as a last resort, after you've already used your powers of observation and context clues to discover what your partner needs.

Try, for instance, the following:

- This seems important. What would be most useful at this moment?

- Would hearing [a different perspective, some advice, a similar experience] help?

- I have some ideas, but I want to make sure I know what you're looking for. Would it be welcome to share [my perspective, advice, etc.]?

- Would it be useful if . . . ?

- Would you like me to listen or respond?

At first, asking clarifying questions can feel awkward. If you are known to be a fairly casual person, asking a friend, "Would you like me to listen or respond?" might seem stilted or foreign coming from your mouth. When asking clarifying questions, remember that the best conversations are the most authentic, so consider these phrases a starting point to help you understand what's needed from you and use your own words.

Notice that these questions do not directly ask your conversation partner "What is it that you need?" or "What do you want from me?," which could sound accusatory as well as put unnecessary pressure on your conversation partner. Instead, they suggest a possible starting point and allow your conversation partner to guide you in the right direction and tell you what they need from there. This is especially useful in relationships where power dynamics or emotions are in play, as it puts control back in the hands of our partners.

Wait for an Opening

Keep in mind that *when* you raise a clarifying question with your conversation partner can have a large impact on how it is received. It may be tempting to ask for role clarification at the beginning of the conversation, but doing so can sound unnatural and derail an otherwise intimate conversation, or arouse suspicion, causing your rapport to quickly evaporate. Other times our conversation partner may not know what they need from us yet, or may not be ready to share it. They may need to talk their way into their need before they can explicitly communicate it. If we push too hard too soon, we can cause them to clam up. Before we launch in to ask what is needed, we should give our conversation partner the space to answer that question for themselves.

In addition, if we become too focused on answering this question, we may inadvertently tune out "irrelevant" information and miss out on what our conversation partner is saying. On the other hand, if we wait too long, we may find ourselves confused, or even frustrated.

Waiting for a break in the conversation is your best bet at getting your conversation partner's intent right. When a natural pause occurs, use a clarifying question to gently ask what is needed (*This seems important. Would it be useful if I shared some advice?*). Your conversation partner may not know the answer until you pose the question. But once you have it, you can respond in kind: whether with validation, support, advice, solutions, or simple gratitude.

Adapt in Real Time

As a licensed therapist in the Bay Area, Tracy McGillis must regularly pick and choose from her tool kit of listening modes depending on what her client needs. "Some people come to therapy with a really deep need to be seen and heard," she told me. "Maybe they grew up in a large family and were temperamentally a more introverted member of that family. If I get the sense that someone needs to take up more space in the room, that that would be particularly therapeutic for them, I really try to sit back a bit and let them take up as much space as they need to. For instance, I try not to jump in with a lot of questions, and maybe paraphrase instead: reflecting back and summarizing what the person's communicating so that the person feels understood."

Most of us are not formally trained, as Tracy is, to quickly adapt to what is needed in the moment. Yet this ability to adjust our behavior for a given situation is something many of us have practice in already: we can learn, for instance, that what is appropriate among friends may not be appropriate at the office, and choose our conversation topics and behavior wisely. If we know we have a tendency to get overzealous when we are passionate about a topic, we can stand by to check ourselves before we go too far. We learn to adapt through experience.

Once you can identify your conversation partner's underlying need, you can adapt your response in real time. For some of us, adapting on a dime is no problem. For others, this will feel like a bit of a stretch. The good news is, the more practice we have pivoting, the easier it gets.

SHIFT MODES

To adapt your default mode to what your conversation partner needs, first acknowledge your understanding of what's needed, and then offer an alternative to how you might typically respond. You can follow a formula like this: "Given that A [need], what if we B [adapted mode]?" For instance:

- I want to celebrate you, but since you're not feeling well, what if we cancel our restaurant reservation instead of forcing it?

- Given you haven't made as much progress as you'd like today, would it help if I watch the kids so you can get some work done?

- Normally I would suggest we power through, but it seems like a break would be welcome. Why don't we hit pause for a minute?

- I know we were planning to work until later, but given what you shared earlier, why don't we take the day off instead?

The best way to show our conversation partners that we understand them is to meet them where they are.

EMPATHETIC LISTENING MEANS LEARNING to USE EVERY SIDE of YOURSELF, NOT just the ONE you ARE MOST COMFORTABLE with

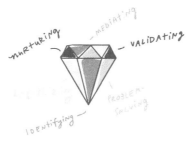

WHEN IN DOUBT, BEAR WITNESS

Kenneth Feinberg has the unenviable position of being the attorney responsible for managing Victim Compensation funds after tragedies like September 11th and the Aurora, Colorado, shooting. He has had many difficult conversations with those dealing with grief and trauma, and learned the hard way the importance—and fragility—of bearing witness. He says:

> I remember at the Pentagon, an 82-year-old man came to see me, tears streaming down his face. And he said to me, 'Mr. Feinberg, I lost my son in the Pentagon. When the plane hit the building, my son escaped safe. But he thought his sister, who also worked in the Pentagon, was trapped. So he went back in to look for her. She had escaped through a side door . . . He died looking for her. Now Mr. Feinberg, my life is over. I'm just going through the motions. A father should never have to bury a son.' And I looked at him, and in an attempt to express empathy I said, 'This is terrible. You lost your son. I know how you feel.' Well, he looked at me. He said, 'Mr. Feinberg, you got a tough job. I don't envy what you have to do, but let me give you a little bit of advice: don't ever tell somebody like me that you know how I feel. You have no idea how I feel, and it's condescending, it's hollow, and it's pretentious. And I wouldn't do it if I were you.' Well I never did that again. You learn the hard way.[1]

Sometimes, despite our best efforts, we may misread a situation. Other times, our conversation partner may just not know what they need, or if they do, they can't (or won't) articulate it. Still other times, we may think we understand but find ourselves striking out. In these cases, our best bet is to simply listen.

Most often, people are just looking to be heard and understood by others. They don't need help—just an empathetic ear to hear them out. This is one of the hardest things to do in conversation, and it can feel unnatural. Most of us do not get much practice just *witnessing*; not taking action can be difficult. But as uncomfortable as this technique may be, sometimes it is exactly what is called for. In allowing others to express themselves and bearing witness to their emotions, we make space for them to fully experience their feelings, without judgment or solutioning.

When in doubt, watch and wait. Look for nonverbal cues such as tensing of the body or tightening of the voice to detect sensitive spots. To help you resist the urge to identify with your conversation partner's experience, bring humility to the fore and remind yourself that their experience is their own. Get curious about your conversation partner's situation and let them lead you in how to be most helpful. Allow them to express themselves fully, and connect to the underlying emotions you've decoded (or they've explicitly expressed). Empathize with their experience without making it about you. Just listening is more than enough.

BEFORE YOU FORGET

Each of us has needs that we bring to a conversation: certain intentions, expectations, or even goals. When we misread or willfully ignore our conversation partner's needs, we can damage the relationship. And when we can't let go of our personal vision for a conversation, others will learn to go elsewhere when what we want is not what they need. Instead of clinging to what we think the conversation should be like, let your conversation partner's needs guide you.

CHAPTER 5

Deepen the Conversation

A research participant was walking me through her work-flow for a study I was conducting on storytelling. We were at her office, a busy newsroom at one of New York's finest journalistic institutions. She clicked through her preferred editing tool for an article in progress while simultaneously scanning the newswire and social media for breaking news. I asked her questions, and she volleyed back efficient answers, scarcely taking her eyes away from her multiscreen setup. I knew within the first few minutes of our interview that it was going to be hard to get—and maintain—her attention, much less a thoughtful and thorough response. I was going to have to make use of every minute we had together, and every question would have to pack a punch.

I was tempted to run through my moderator's guide—a list of questions and activities I had prepared to ensure I walked away with the right intel for the team at headquarters—and to take whatever answers came my way. At least that way, I could reason, I'd be sure to get through them all. But I knew from experience that I'd walk away with a whole lot of nothing if I took that approach: I would get only high-level responses, without much depth. My interview subject's training could only make things even harder. Reporters, perhaps unsurprisingly, are very good at giving only what they want to reveal—they are practiced in getting information from others, so are often quick to guard their own information. To truly get to know her, I needed to break through her attention and protective shield. So I pruned my list and focused on fewer, but more impactful, questions.

When the participant showed me a story she found worth telling, I dove in: "What does a good story look like?"

"You just know," she said, and I had to follow up.

"How do you know?"

"You feel it in your gut."

I persisted: "What does that feel like?"

"Like a rush. Like you're discovering something new, conquering uncharted territory. Like a pioneer." OK, now we were getting somewhere.

"What makes territory uncharted?" I asked.

"I typically look for something unique—something that hasn't been said before, either because it hasn't been covered and I'm the first to say *anything* on the matter or, in many cases, because I'm the first to say *this thing* on the matter. Uncharted doesn't mean it's untouched, but it does mean there is something new to say about it," she explained.

Now I had something to work with: a philosophy this beat reporter stood by, a clear point of view. With a few examples of stories she was proud of, I could easily gain an understanding of both her strategy and her execution.

If you look at the questions I asked in this scenario, you'll notice a lot of questions that begin with "What" and "How." What I didn't ask were "When" and "Who" questions, which would have likely yielded dead end responses ("Every morning," "my editor"). And none were set up to elicit a mere "Yes" or "No." Each question I asked was an invitation to share more. I was asking what I call *connecting questions*.

Connecting Questions Help Us Go Deeper

Connecting questions are questions, and sometimes statements, neutrally framed to elicit an open response, without suggesting or biasing toward a particular reply. They give our conversation partners the wiggle room to answer as much or as little as they'd like—without projecting our experience or assumptions onto them. When our conversation partner is shy, they are a gentle way to encourage them to open up. When they are guarded, they are an honest way to show them they have nothing to be afraid of. When we can sense that our conversation partner has more to say, but for whatever reason—fear, politeness, ambivalence—they aren't going there, they are a warm reassurance that they are safe with us. Whether your conversation partner is a close friend or a new teammate, connecting questions open paths to greater understanding of each other, and greater intimacy as a result. The benefit is that you do not know where the answer will take you—which, if you are in the business of exploring someone's mind, is the perfect place to start.

Therapists, for example, frequently employ connecting questions in their clinical practice. They might ask, "Tell me about your relationships at work" or "How did it make you feel when that happened?" Both prompt the client to share how they're feeling, what their beliefs are, and what values they hold, without cornering them into a specific response, and instead guiding them past the surface to understand what some of the core, root issues or emotions driving their behavior might be.

CONNECTiNG QUEStiONS hElp us Go DEEPER

Of course, we should always honor what our conversation partner is willing to share—there are many valid reasons to hold back in conversation. Sometimes time and space are what's needed; other times safety and trust have not yet been sufficiently established. Our goal with these questions is not to needlessly press, pry, or push others to open up—in addition to making others uncomfortable, unwelcome prodding can backfire. Our conversation partner may feel pressured to share more than they are comfortable with and regret the outcome later on (*I wish I hadn't said that. How did that happen?*). They may adopt an adversarial stance to fight back if it feels like we are forcing their hand (*He is really trying to get me to admit my fears. Well, good luck buddy, that's not going to happen.*). They may begin to feel that you are more interested in gathering information than really understanding them (*Why is she suddenly so interested in me? Is she trying to get my vote for her promotion?*). If your conversation partner stays mum despite your encouragement, it's worth reflecting on what cues you may have missed.

Assuming you have permission, there are three types of connecting questions you'll want to leverage in conversation: exploratory questions, encouraging questions, and reflection questions.

EXPLORATORY QUESTIONS

One of my best researchers was having a tough interview. The participant had asked to move her session at the very last minute (a no-no in the research world), and thirty minutes later than expected, she signed into the video call. Despite the late start, the conversation kicked off smoothly: researcher and participant got to know each other, and from the back room you could see the conversation was flowing. We were learning about the participant's professional goals and future aspirations, and the team was hanging on to every word. But then, a cell phone pinged.

Ping! Ping! Ping! Our participant was a popular lady. Her phone was blowing up. Though we hope that in a session we will have the participant's undivided attention (and typically compensate them for their time to incentivize good behavior), it doesn't always turn out that way. Rather than mute her phone or put it away, our participant had begun to answer her messages mid-session. She tried to hide her texting, but it was obvious what was happening. Ever a trooper, my researcher kept her spirits high, repeating questions the participant had been too distracted to hear, staying calm and polite despite the participant's multitasking. She gently persisted, the definition of grace under fire.

The problem was, the pings didn't stop. Fifteen minutes later, the participant no longer bothered hiding her phone from view, now texting in the open. Maybe because the session was over video conference, she felt particularly daring in her multitasking, and free to prioritize her messages above our time together. Or perhaps we were truly boring her. Either way, it wasn't pretty. I could tell my researcher's energy was waning, and the back room was getting antsy, too.

Sensing rapport was slipping, my researcher began to speed things up. She raced through the rest of her questions, ticking them off one by one. And in her haste, she began to rely on questions that narrowed, and sometimes biased, the participant's response to get the job done. Instead of asking the participant, "What are your thoughts on the prototype overall?" she asked, "Do you prefer the first screen or the second screen?" This could be perceived as an efficient approach, but the question skipped over some important information—it mistakenly assumed the participant liked at least *one* of the screens, when in fact, she may not have liked either of them. And instead of keeping things exploratory and asking, "How, if at all, could you see yourself using this feature?" she asked the more close-ended question, "Would you use this?" A yes or no would technically answer my researcher's question, but she would not likely learn why the participant chose that answer. The researcher missed out on asking what I call *exploratory questions*.

Usually beginning with "how" and "what," exploratory questions are unbiased: they neither presume an answer up front, nor do they suggest a binary outcome (yes or no). Another way of describing this structure is *open-ended*. A true open-ended question can lead us down many possible and unexpected paths, because they allow our conversation partner to interpret the question as they see fit; when they do, they may give us more or different information than expected. Overall, exploratory questions help us to see the full picture by releasing our conversation partners from expectations, assumptions, or hypotheses we may have about them.

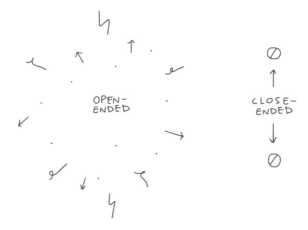

Take, for instance, the following exploratory questions:

- How do you feel about that?

- What does "ideal" look like?

- How would you approach . . . ?

- What would you do if . . . ?

- What's the biggest risk to . . . ?

What would have happened if the researcher had asked exploratory questions? Instead of simply learning *if* a feature might be used, she could get to the "Whys," "Why nots," and "Hows" that would have provided her with a more complete and accurate understanding of what the participant really thought of our prototype.

In day-to-day conversations, exploratory questions can be used to break the ice at a cocktail party, reconnect with an old friend, get to know your colleagues better, or even strengthen family ties. With practice, asking can become second nature. The more you use exploratory questions, the richer your conversations become.

ENCOURAGING PHRASES

I first spoke to Leslie about her meal-planning process for research I was conducting on cooking routines. At the start of our chat, she was excited to share her process, animated and quick to laugh as she told me about her favorite cookbooks and family recipes. But when we started talking about grocery shopping, she began to withdraw. Her speech softened and slowed. The more I asked her about her time in the store, the more guarded she became. I was losing her with every passing minute.

Though I wanted to let her off the hook, I couldn't. I desperately needed these learnings to help my cross-functional team set the right strategy and build the right product. Instead, I began to ask smaller and smaller questions, questions that did not even *sound* like questions. When she shared that she tried to keep grocery store shopping efficient, I asked her to say more. When she mentioned she preferred morning shopping to evening, I encouraged her to walk me through what that looked like. A few barely there, encouraging phrases helped her finally share that in fact, grocery shopping was a nightmare: there weren't enough coupons for what she really wanted to buy, mega supermarkets had layouts that could confuse the best of us, and having to bring the children along could quickly turn an otherwise ordinary errand into a hair-raising experience. Embarrassed by the tantrums and penny-pinching, Leslie had initially held back on sharing details. But with a little bit of encouragement, she let out a sigh of relief and confessed that she would *love* to skip that step of meal-planning altogether. I was able to avoid a total shutdown simply by asking her to share more.

Exploratory questions can help us further a conversation, but sometimes our conversation partners need an extra nudge. If you can tell that your conversation partner wants (or even needs) to share but isn't sure how, they may need your encouragement. Encouraging phrases gently open a path for our conversation partner to say more. Sometimes all they need is to be asked to keep talking, so they can continue processing and working on things aloud.

Encouraging phrases sound like:

- Say more about that.
- Tell me what this means to you.
- Walk me through . . .
- Tell me more.
- What else?

Other encouraging phrases are even more subtle. With a well-timed pause, these statements can serve as a small encouragement for our conversation partner to keep going. Because they invite our conversation partner to expand on an idea or feeling, I call these types of encouraging phrases *expansion prompts*. For instance:

- It sounds like that was difficult for you. [*pause*]

- It seems like that was very exciting for you. [*pause*]
- You feel that way because . . . [*pause*]

These phrases work when we share a simple observation and prompt our conversation partner to expand on it. For instance, we can articulate the sentiment expressed by our conversation partner and then give them the space to respond to or build on it. As we learned in chapter 2, a brief pause can go a long way to subtly encourage our conversation partners to say more.

These simple but powerful phrases pulled more than their weight in unlocking insights in my conversation with Leslie, and they can be leveraged in personal and professional conversations, too. For the friend who doesn't wear his heart on his sleeve and just lost a parent, encouraging phrases can give him the space to safely share what he needs without pushing him too far. For the colleague on the edge of giving her peer some much-needed feedback, these encouragements can give her the permission to go there. For the single parent trying to keep it all together, so, too, can these phrases provide a necessary outlet for the burden he carries. Whether our conversation partner is hesitant to be forthright due to temperament (naturally reticent), circumstance (in need of time or space to process their thoughts), or emotion (deterred by shame or pride), these small nudges help us to peel back the layers and deepen a conversation, without pushing anyone too far.

REFLECTION QUESTIONS

Stella was one of my strongest researchers. Extremely organized and ever resourceful, she could reliably complete any project sent her way. A natural community builder, she was well liked on the team and often sought out additional work to help her teammates. She had already spearheaded a number of initiatives to make the team more effective.

The problem was, Stella didn't see herself as the rock star she was. And in her eagerness to help others, she sometimes had a hard time saying no, even when she had her hands full. In a one-on-one, she shared wanting to take on a project for the team. *Great*, I thought, and was curious to hear more about the kinds of projects she was interested in. She didn't have any ideas, she said, she just wanted to help. As her manager, she was hoping I could suggest some projects the group could benefit from. I did have some ideas—though for fairly unsexy administrative tasks, like budget tracking and contract filing. These would indeed help the team, but I had a feeling this wasn't what Stella was looking for. Stella's strength and joy was in bringing people together—paperwork probably wasn't going to cut it.

When you have a high performer, you really want to keep them happy, so it was important to me to make sure we picked the right project. But Stella being Stella, she immediately signed herself up for one of the thankless jobs I had mentioned while thinking aloud. That's when I started to slow things down and ask some questions: I wanted to be sure she found a project that would be motivating and exciting to her, not one that just happened to be available.

I asked an exploratory question to start: "What kind of impact are you hoping to make?" She wanted to help relieve some pressure for her teammates, she said. A start, but we would need more to work from, so I used an encouraging phrase from there: "Say more about that." She shared that the team seemed overworked and over-tired. She wanted to take more on to remove some of the burden, and the project I'd mentioned sounded like a great way of doing that. Getting warmer, but with more detail we could do even better.

I pressed on for more specificity, this time presenting an either-or scenario for Stella to respond to. "Is it that you'd like to provide a morale boost or project relief?" I asked. It was definitely project relief. "Is it more about working in the shadows or in the spotlight?" Shadows, for sure. "Is it about deepening your existing skill set or acquiring a new one?" That, she would have to think about. And when she did, we ended up going with an entirely different project.

This slightly more directed set of questions helped us both gain clarity on what Stella was looking for. Because they provoke reflection, I call them *reflection questions*, and bring them out to complement the work encouraging phrases and exploratory questions do. Though encouraging questions can pack a punch, from time to time our conversation partners may need room for additional contemplation. It's not always easy for us to share our thoughts on the spot, even when we want to.

Reflection questions work by directly prompting our conversation partner to think through the topic at hand, typically through comparison. When we put options in front of our conversation partner, we invite them to reflect on which, if any, are closest to the sentiment they are trying to express—whether your direct report is struggling to think through their immediate projects or future career goals, your sibling is spinning on how to celebrate their birthday, or a friend can't decide if he wants to have kids or not. This can be very helpful, since oftentimes, even if we can't articulate what we *want*, we know with certainty what we *don't* want. Having a few options to choose from can help bring those feelings, preferences, and opinions to light.

If you've ever listened to the public radio program and podcast *This American Life*, you've heard this tactic in action. Ira Glass is its iconic host and storyteller, and he is a master of this technique. "Sometimes you have to theorize what the answer might be," he says. "I find myself in a lot of interviews saying, 'Well is it more like this or is it like this? I can imagine it would be this way or this way. What is it?' And then they're forced to kind of go somewhere—to bat away one of your theories and to run at one of the others."[1]

When using reflection questions, you'll want to be careful not to offer more than one either-or pairing at a time. If we offer more than that (*is it A, B, C, or D?*), we may inadvertently send our conversation partner into indecision paralysis and leave them spinning more than before.[2]

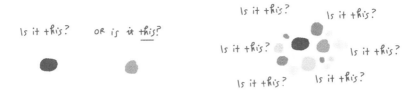

The questions below provide a starting point for reflection without overwhelming our conversation partner.

- Are you looking for something action-packed or low-key?
- Would you call this feedback a must-have or a nice-to-have?
- Would you say you feel more frustrated or disappointed?
- Is it more about wanting a raise or wanting to be recognized?
- Is it more like Mussolini or a tree? (This last one is a great word-guessing game for long car rides. You have to think about it, a lot.)

Each of these questions provides a possible path forward for our conversation partner. Though they use a close-ended structure, they are the exception that can further open—rather than close—a conversation. They are designed to extend a line of inquiry rather than to confirm and conclude it. Most people will naturally provide more than a one-word response to these kinds of questions.

Disconnecting Questions

Remember the researcher at the beginning of this chapter who faced a multitasking participant? In her haste to get through a painful session, she missed a chance at getting a more complete and accurate picture of what the participant really thought of our prototype. For the sake of time, she led with her assumptions, relying on *discon-necting questions* to get her through the session.

A disconnecting question is a question designed to elicit a specific response based on what the asker believes (or desires) the answer to be, and can be used to drive particular outcomes and decisions—to make a sale, get to "yes," prove a point, or even escape a nose-diving research session. Like projecting, disconnecting questions keep us in our own experience and assumptions. They can *feel* like they are about connecting, but deep down they are not. Rather, they *fish* for a point of connection or *lead* others to express a need they may not actually have. They *expose* a problem to be solved and attempt to *diagnose* a solution (conveniently, whatever the speaker is selling, seeking agreement on, or even raising money for).

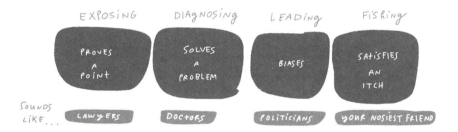

The examples below show what I mean:

- Are you upset? (Assumption: You're upset.)

- Do you think that's a problem? (Assumption: You think that's a problem.)

- Does that mean you don't like it? (Assumption: You don't like it.)

- Which prototype do you like better? (Assumption: You like one of these prototypes.)

Each question is *close-ended*, meaning it elicits single-word responses—most often, yes or no. This is precisely as intended: when we want to confirm a belief or hypothesis, teeing up a limited number or kind of response works in our favor. Not all close-ended questions are disconnecting (recall reflecting questions), but when we combine a close-ended question with a self-serving intent, as these questions often do, we land on a disconnecting question.

Sometimes we employ disconnecting questions deliberately, but usually they emerge out of habit or haste, as they did with the researcher. We don't mean to steer our conversation partner in a particular direction, but if we're not paying attention, we might say to our direct report, "I'm guessing you are too busy to take this project on, right?" instead of asking, "What is your workload like these days?" and giving them the chance to take on a stretch project. If our partner seems upset, we might say, "Do you want some alone time to recover?" instead of asking, "What would be most helpful to you right now?" and giving them a chance to ask for what they need. If our roommate seems tired, we presume, "You're too tired to go out, right?" instead of asking, "What do you feel like doing tonight?" and letting them tell us what kind of Friday they're up for.

In the end, these questions elicit only partial or inaccurate answers, tainted by our suggestions and biases. If you lead your conversation partner—or, in research, your participant—to the answer you want to hear, your "data" is effectively useless.

DISCONNECTING QUESTIONS SUGGEST WE KNOW WHERE TO GO

GET ON BOARD

CONFIRM MY BIAS

THIS WAY

FOLLOW ME

PROVE MY POINT

Whether in the lab or in real life, disconnecting questions prevent us from learning the truth—and can sometimes lead to tears. They can engender miscommunication (*That's not what I meant!*), ill will (*You've twisted my words.*), and misunderstanding (*You don't get me at all if you're asking that.*). They can cause hurt (*I can't believe this person thinks that about me.*) and alienation (*I thought you knew me better than that.*). And when questions are obviously self-serving, people commonly self-protect and withhold entirely. Above all, if we can't learn the truth our conversation partner has to say, it will be very hard to authentically connect with them.

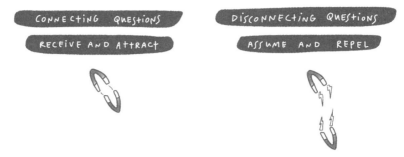

Reframe Your Questions

So how do we go from reflexively asking disconnecting questions to intentionally asking connecting ones? First, check yourself for assumptions or beliefs you might be inadvertently baking into your questions. Try to step away from close-ended "Is," "Are," and Do" questions that assume an outcome, and instead use "How" and "What" to make your questions more open-ended.

Consider the possibilities for connection that can arise when we reframe the questions below.

- Instead of asking "Was it tough being the first researcher on the team?" (Assumption: It must have been hard to do everything by yourself.), try "What was it like to be the first researcher on the team?"

- Instead of asking "So you want kids because you're getting older?" (Assumption: You must be desperate to get pregnant by now.), try "What draws you to having a family now?"

- Instead of asking "Did that meeting upset you?" (Assumption: You don't seem happy with how that went.), try "How do you think that meeting went?"

You'll notice that in the above examples, I've shied away from asking "Why." Though you can very easily turn disconnecting questions' close-ended structure into an open-ended structure by asking "Why," it's best not to. Unlike "How" and "What" questions, "Why" questions can sound judgmental to our ears. Repeatedly asking "Why?" can also feel like an invasion of privacy. At the risk of having your curiosity confused for condescension or nosiness, limit your use of "Why" questions and stick to "How," "What," or "Tell me . . ." questions instead.

Right on, let's practice.

EXERCISE:
Transform Disconnecting
Questions into Connecting Ones

Grab a notebook and transform the following "Is," "Are," and Do" questions to "How" and "What" to make them more connecting.

- Are you nervous about your presentation?
- Do you get along with your boss?
- Is your team happy?
- Does that make you feel sad?
- Do you have a good relationship with your parents?
- Are you mad at me?

BEFORE YOU FORGET

So much of how we move through the world is by habit, including how we ask questions. But the disconnecting questions we often rely on can backfire and keep us in our own experience. If you're tired of getting one-word responses from your partner, colleague, lover, or sibling, it's time to start asking a different kind of question. With connecting questions, we can go beyond the superficial and get to know our conversation partner much more deeply.

CHAPTER 6

Stay Flexible

A researcher on my team was conducting a study on news-reading habits. As with all studies, he had prepared a set of questions in advance, and in a session, he starts by covering the basics: "What are some of the topics you follow online?" The participant is naturally chatty and says, "I read a lot of business news, and I love following politics. It's like watching a drama unfold—there are so many characters to keep track of, not to mention the tug-of-war over policy, too. I'm constantly on my phone, catching up on the latest while I'm commuting, during a break at work, or at home. Honestly, I even read in the bathroom! I probably shouldn't read as much news as I do, but I really can't help it."

From the back room where I'm observing the session, my ears perk up. Though we're only a few minutes into the interview, the participant's instant candor makes it clear we don't need any more warm-up questions. She's offered us early insight into her news-reading routine (always on), which is exactly what we want to learn about. Her openness gives us permission to jump ahead in our list of questions and explore—to save us time and effort and get to the heart of our session.

Improvising in this way would also signal that we are listening: there's no need for more introductory questions because she's been so forthcoming already. In fact, continuing on this same path could come across as unfocused, aloof, or even disrespectful. That's why I hope to hear the researcher probe deeper: to follow this thread, see where it goes, and what it might teach us about this participant's news-reading habits. A well-placed "Tell me more" could do the trick.

Instead, the researcher misses his opening. He is so focused on getting through his script that he doesn't really *hear* the participant and moves on rather than personalizing his approach. "Great," he says, "and when did you start following these topics?" The participant leans back in her seat. "Probably a few years ago," she says, and begins to absentmindedly investigate her nail bed. The door closes for a far less important detail that happened to be the next question on his list.

Sometimes, without realizing it, we may get tunnel vision in conversation. Like the researcher, we may be so driven to meet a goal or get to the bottom of something that we forget to look up, take a breath, and listen to what our conversation partner is actually saying. It can also happen when we are too afraid to try something different, or too attached to our own point of view. Though it can be useful to set an intention and even devise a plan to get there, when we stick to these too strictly, we often miss the signs that change is called for. When we aren't flexible, we run the risk of misinterpreting others, discouraging them from sharing more, or missing the chance to evolve our thinking for the better.

To stay connected in conversation, we must be ready to learn from what's in front of us and loosen our scripts, get comfortable with the zigs, zags, and even awkward silences that make our conversations unique, and adjust as we go. If none of these suffice, we may need to let go of our plans entirely and start anew.

Loosen the Script

There are some conversations we prepare for—a performance review, a session with a client, an intervention with a friend, or even a first date—that don't go as expected. We may have a carefully crafted agenda for a meeting that we find no longer holds, a set of ideas we wish to pitch but find are unwelcome, a meticulously planned speech that is met with willful ignorance, or an intention to get to know someone that is thwarted by their self-protective nature. When this happens, it's important that we know how to navigate the new landscape.

The best interviewers know that sometimes it's wise to go "off script"—to keep sight of a goal or hold an intention in conversation but to stay flexible on how we get there. If we want to understand our client's needs to deliver an amazing project, we may need to shave a few unplanned minutes off our packed agenda for rapport-building small talk. If we hope to counsel someone through a difficult time, we need to be attuned to what feels supportive to them and open to changing course if our approach is not helpful. If our intention is to get to know someone better, we need to give them the space to move at their own pace. The trick is to not get too attached to our script: to stay flexible and to adjust when change is called for. Doing so gives others the room to surprise us, prove us wrong, teach us, and let us get to know them.

This is especially true in high-stakes conversations, like job interviews, negotiations, mediations, or even marriage proposals. While preparing what we will say in advance can be a helpful starting point, and even give us the confidence we need to take these sometimes intimidating conversations on, leaning too much on preplanned remarks can get us into trouble. A job candidate spitting out canned responses will hardly sound authentic, and a negotiation can't be successful without a give-and-take to find something that works for both sides. No mediation comes without compromise, and hardly any marriage proposal goes exactly as envisioned, either (which often makes for a better story anyway). If we don't adjust our sails, it will be difficult to connect.

To keep a connection open or revive one that is flickering out, you'll need to loosen your script. If you get too hung up on what to say or ask next, you may miss what your conversation partner is trying to say. Instead, we can strike a balance: we can keep our script in mind just enough to keep the discussion moving in the right direction, without becoming completely beholden to it and forcing a conversation.

Try not to overplan what you're going to say

Aim for a North Star,   Not a checklist

To do this, you can:

- **Incorporate new information.** If we cling to existing knowledge—of our conversation partner's feelings, intentions, mood, or point of view—without making way for new understanding, we may be perceived as stubborn, out of touch, inflexible, or even ignorant. Give others a chance to surprise and inform your thinking in conversation. Make the necessary space to receive new information: show your conversation partner you are listening through nonverbals like eye contact and nodding, and by expressing affirmations (*Yes, go on.*). Pay attention to your conversation partner's behavior—verbal and nonverbal—and incorporate these cues as you determine your response.

- **Reassess as you go.** Given the information you're taking in, is your current "script" still the right one, or is a pivot appropriate? Gut check whether your next set of questions or even responses remain relevant given what you have learned already. Keep questions and ideas on hand to further the conversation, but be open to exploration, too.

- **Look for cues that you are heading in the right direction.** As you loosen your script, continue to monitor your conversation partner's response. Are they receptive, or do they seem to be lost, distracted, or even frustrated? This, too, should inform your approach, and where the conversation goes next.

Build on Each Other's Ideas

One of the easiest ways to stay open in conversation and let things unfold as they must is to build on others' ideas. Improv comedians are masters of this technique. To successfully pull off a joke, they must be hyperfocused on the scene at hand and ready to incorporate and add to any idea that comes their way. They need to not only remain open to what their fellow troupe members put forward but also trust that they are heading in the right direction. If you're performing improv, the last thing you want to do is be caught off guard, stuck in your own thoughts, and unable to contribute to the current scene.

That's where "Yes, and . . ." comes in. "Yes, and" is a mechanism used to let scenes go where they need to go. When a character, scenario, or other detail is introduced in a scene, responding "yes, and" instead of "no, but" allows troupe members to collaboratively design the scene. If, for example, a member of the group sets up a scene to include, say, a gorilla, the others will say *"yes, and . . . that gorilla is an excellent singer."* This "yes, and" mentality is at the core of what makes a good scene and why improv is often characterized by unexpected comedic twists and turns. "Yes, and" is about faith that the troupe is heading in the right direction and collaborating to get there together.

"Yes, and" can work wonders in conversation, too. With this mindset, we don't take for granted our conversation partner's ideas; we take them as building blocks for conversation instead. This is particularly helpful when brainstorming new ideas with others, debating the pros and cons of a given scenario, looking to compromise with a partner, or finding middle ground with a prickly teammate.

A "yes, and" mindset sounds like:

- Let's start with that. What else?
- Let's build from there.
- I can understand that. And also . . .
- True! And . . .

Learn from Conversation Detours

Some of the best conversations often end miles from where they started. When a conversation really flows, time flies and we can easily go down a rabbit hole with our conversation partner. Sometimes, the unexpected twists and turns in conversation are as random as a word association game, and they provide an entertaining glimpse of what it's like to be inside our conversation partner's brain. But more often than not, these detours are less random than they appear. Someone may be avoiding a difficult topic, taking the conversation left and right to get around broaching it (*That's the third time my direct report has stalled on telling me how his project is going.*). Or, they may feel they need permission to talk about something and use a roundabout path to get there, like subtly bringing up their philosophy on screen time and kids when someone shows off the newest iPhone. Then again, they may think they are talking about what's on their minds, only to find they needed to talk through a superficial problem or topic to get to a deeper one (*So this wasn't about where you want to go on vacation? This was about how you don't like your job?*). Or maybe these detours are a sign that our conversation partner is bored, and over it—whatever subject of conversation "it" might be. Reasons for detours may vary, but one thing is clear: these unpredictable twists and turns are signals to pay attention.

Detours can sound like:

- "What-if" lines of thinking (hypotheticals, daydreams, etc.)
- "Speaking of . . ." pivots

- Aha moments

- Non sequiturs (illogical responses that do not follow the topic at hand)

You may not immediately know the cause of a given detour, but sticking with it will help you discover its purpose. When they surface, do your best to move forward with your conversation partner and let them lead the way. It's OK not to return to where you started—right away, or ever—you may have already landed exactly where you needed to be. Instead, use the detour presented to you as your new starting point for understanding your conversation partner (*If my direct report isn't willing to ask for help to move his project forward, we might need more trust to get there.*). Having this new information will make any return to your original topic more fruitful, too (*Now that he is broaching the subject, I'm going to move forward gently to understand what happened.*).

Get Comfortable with Silence

My team and I were testing out a prototype for a new product that would change how people used our website. The prototype wasn't perfect—that was the point. We knew it was half-baked and needed a lot of work: The navigation was confusing, links were broken, and we had pulled out some of the site's basic functionality. The prototype was purposefully unfinished and "out there" to help us glean people's reactions to the idea of the thing rather than the finished, polished product.

During a session, I made an excuse to leave the participant, Edmarc, alone in the research lab for a few minutes after instructing him to poke around the prototype. I wanted to see how he would react without me watching over his shoulder. I joined my teammates in the back room, where they watched from behind what looked to the participant to be a mirror, and we held our breath. Edmarc rightly tapped on what should have been links, but weren't. He tried to tap through to a website, but couldn't. He was able to take some basic actions in the app, but many did not come easily. From the back room, the prototype looked like a disaster.

I went back to join Edmarc and asked him what he thought of the prototype. "It's cool," he said, employing a broad statement. "I'm into it." I reminded myself not to be surprised. It's common for participants to want to give the "right" answer to please their interviewer. Despite what Edmarc had told me, it was clear that he found the prototype confusing. How could I encourage him to say what he *really* thought, rather than what he thought I wanted to hear? Sure, I could ask him directly, but doing so could bias him to focus strictly on the negative. It might also embarrass him to know I could see through his overly flattering language, and inadvertently curb the conversation. I needed a balanced, honest assessment, untainted by me, the moderator.

Sometimes the best way of letting a conversation go where it needs to go, instead of where *we* think it should go, is by exercising a little self-restraint. So I repeated Edmarc's assessment back to him, employing an encouraging question to see if he might share his honest opinion.

"So you're into it," I said, using his words to see if he'd bite.

"Yep," he said, and left it at that. Then I began to silently count to ten. Most people will rush to fill the void before ten seconds are up. Some may push it to fifteen, even twenty. But in general, if you can train yourself to stay silent for a hair longer than is comfortable, it's likely your conversation partner will jump in to fill the void. When they do jump in, it'll be worth the wait.

I didn't get past seven when Edmarc chimed in, "Well, actually, I like that you can still find what you're looking for, but it was kind of hard to organize it afterward." There it was—an opening into honest feedback. That, I could work with.

Most of us feel compelled to talk in the company of others. Silence between interlocutors is uncommon and uncomfortable, so instead of letting it hang between us, we change topics, we overshare, or, when we are out of ways to fill the air, we even make excuses to part ways. If a question we pose is not immediately answered, we may get discouraged and quickly chime in to drive things forward. If a conversation starts to stall, we may suspect our conversation partner has lost interest and begin to wrap things up to let them (and ourselves) off the hook. If a beat passes in conversation and no one speaks up, it must be time to move on.

But silence, if you can sit with it, can be very powerful in conversation. Silence opens the space between us. Silence can indicate: You have the floor. Do with it what you will. Take the time you need to. I am here when you are ready to say more.

Perhaps your conversation partner hasn't lost interest in the topic at hand but is carefully formulating her thoughts before sharing them. If a beat passes and no one speaks up, your conversation partner may simply be gearing up to speak. Your question may not have been about to go unanswered—it may have just needed to marinate a moment longer. Sometimes when it appears we have run out of things to say, we are just getting started.

To hear our partners in these moments, we have to give them the space to enter the conversation. That means pausing and stopping ourselves from hastily moving on or changing the subject when the occasional silence has us squirming in our seats.

Change Up Your Surroundings

Sometimes, staying flexible looks like taking a conversation out of the rigid, fluorescent-lit walls of the office, conference room, or classroom and out into the world—though the sidewalk around your building will work just fine. At my first job in Silicon Valley, I discovered the joys of the walking one-on-one. Some of the best conversations with my manager took place while we were walking, strolling around a pond outside our office, just shaded enough to keep us cool in the summer and warm in the fall. We took slow but purposeful laps as we discussed both the menial and the hard stuff: work-in-flight, performance expectations, and work relationship conflicts. It was a relief to not have to be in our generic, stuffy conference rooms, but it was also helpful to not be seated across from each other—unnaturally formal and unintentionally adversarial, as if in battle. When the conversation would turn to a difficult place, it felt a lot easier to broach those subjects as we walked side by side, instead of inadvertently staring each other down.

A change in your environment can help you and others share what might otherwise be difficult to express. Below are some simple ways to do that:

- **Get moving.** Taking leisurely walks with my manager provided a welcome change from our routine in conversation. Having continuous motion, as when we are hiking, driving, or otherwise moving, is especially helpful to facilitating open conversation; as the scene refreshes itself, so do we.

- **Venture outdoors.** A change of scenery can reset our energy levels and activate a different kind of thinking. Getting out into nature is especially useful. Try a park or leafy area near your office or dwelling if you can, which has been shown to improve our moods.[1]

- **Break eye contact.** Try activities that give you an excuse to rest your eyes outside the contours of your conversation partner's face. This might seem counterintuitive, since eye contact can helpfully signal we are present and receptive to our conversation partner. But sometimes, breaking eye contact can actually be beneficial, especially when talking about sensitive topics, since both parties are free to take a breather when they need one. Having an important conversation while taking in a baseball game together, for instance, or grabbing a kitchen-facing table at a restaurant for your discussion can give both parties a chance to look elsewhere, and get vulnerable.

- **Occasional, not often.** Save too many uncomfortable conversations for a long car ride with your partner, and you will both begin to resent road trips. Cut out eye contact altogether, and you may begin to feel ignored. Avoid having difficult conversations face-to-face entirely, and trust can begin to crumble. Use the environment around you as a way to recharge in conversation from time to time, but be careful not to overdo it.

Let Go of the Plan

It was supposed to be a one-on-one session. I dialed in to the video call and waited for my participant to enter. Marcel's face popped up, and I launched into my preamble, telling her what to expect from our time together, and that I was eager to learn about her work and later have her pressure test our prototype. But before we could dive in, another face popped up. And another, and another, and still another—and in less than a minute, five faces filled my screen.

"Meet the team, Ximena!" Marcel said as she introduced me to

Gael from Creative, Ellie from Social, and so on, and so on. "I know you said you wanted to talk through my workflow, but since I only do the strategy part, I figured it made sense to invite everyone else, too!" It was a generous thought, but it took me off track. How could I test my prototype with five people on the line at once, only one of whom might ever actually use our product day-to-day?

"Oh!" I said, "Hello!"

Though I would have preferred to send co-workers 2 through 5 off, I couldn't. Marcel's team represented a big account for us, one that was high on our list of clients to retain. I couldn't risk appearing rude or disappointing them. After all, they were here to help, even if it would be slightly . . . unhelpful.

The thought of proceeding through sixty minutes of organized chaos was daunting. I had never facilitated a session this large before, much less adapted my protocol so drastically at the last minute. And with everyone on video conference, it was bound to get messy. But I would have to abandon the old plan and come up with a new one on the spot. I needed to retool our session in real time.

Often, even a little flexibility can go a long way to making the most of our time together; making small changes, like the ones discussed earlier, can help us maneuver conversations to meet our partner where they are. But sometimes, a more drastic change is necessary, and our plan requires radical alterations in order for us to truly understand each other.

"Thanks everyone for coming," I said. "Here's how this is going to work." We would do lightning round intros, enough for me to understand who everyone was so that I could modify my questions accordingly and pitch them to the right person. Not everyone would get a chance to answer each question, I told them, but everyone would be asked *some* questions. And when we got to the prototype, I'd need help primarily from the person who used this tool day-to-day; for everyone else, I'd love their opinion, too—after. "Sound OK?" I asked, and the team nodded. "Great," I said. "Let's get started."

In our quest to connect with others, we must leave room for flexibility and let our conversation partners go at their own pace, and in their own way. When our plan has changed drastically, it may be necessary to throw it out entirely and learn from what's in front of us. When Marcel brought her team onto the line, I learned a lot about her—that she is a team player, highly collaborative, and so good at her job that she scarcely recognizes the work she does as important enough on its own. By staying flexible, I was able to honor Marcel's direction and still learn the answers to the questions I had.

Letting go of the plan is especially useful when we have a meeting agenda that must suddenly be adapted to accommodate last-minute changes, a discussion unexpectedly turns into an argument, a celebrated work anniversary turns into a somber farewell, a one-on-one with a direct report kicks off with an announcement that they are quitting the team, or other surprising twists are thrown our way. In these moments, it won't make sense to follow the usual routine. Instead, you can:

- **Embrace the unknown.** Prepare to be surprised and don't try to keep things tidy. Roll with the punches as they come, and you'll learn much more about your conversation partner and what's needed.

- **Show your support.** If your conversation partner takes things in an unexpected direction, honor that and adapt with them. We can show them we are supportive of their new direction by acknowledging we have heard their need to shift gears and committing to their decision. Phrases such as "I understand you'd prefer to . . . Let's do that now" or "Outside of X and Y, what else needs to happen?" can help.

- **Don't ask the same question twice.** Asking the same question twice tells your conversation partner that you remain stuck on the old plan and are unable to change course (*Are you sure you want to . . . ? Still sure? How about now?*). Not only will this frustrate your conversation partner, but it also shows them you are not listening. If you are about to ask the same question again, stop to ask yourself if you really don't know the answer, or if this is a sign you're not yet on board with the conversation's new direction.

BEFORE YOU FORGET

To tap into our greatest empathetic selves, we need to stay flexible and open in conversation. When our conversation takes a detour or does not go as expected, throwing away our script can get us closer to the connection we are looking for. Our conversations may look different than we'd imagined, but they'll still be just as meaningful as, if not more meaningful than, before.

CHAPTER 7

Confirm Your Comprehension

My team and I were conducting field research on how people shop, and each participant had agreed to host us in their home for an afternoon. We would be spending a whopping three hours together at each site, so we tried to keep things interactive.

Marta, one of our participants, showed us some of her most recent purchases: shoes made from recycled material from a trendy local start-up, lipstick made with all-natural ingredients and absolutely no animal testing, denim made in the United States, and an expensive but beautifully crafted jacket with hand stitching and embroidered details. As an artist herself, Marta explained, she valued craftsmanship in design—and was willing to pay for it. She also regularly read up on brands of interest before purchasing and made sure the businesses she shopped at shared similar values to her own.

The closet walk-through complete, we now had just a few formal questions for Marta before returning to the office. We showed her our prototype and asked her to try it out. Oliver, the product manager in charge of bringing this product to life, was particularly excited about leveraging a voice-activation feature in our prototype (*We can help people shop hands-free!*), but given what Marta had told us of her shopping process, I suspected it might be a little too newfangled for her purposes; we would have to wait and see.

Marta made her way through our prototype and was fairly positive in her feedback. She preferred a larger image so she could better see the details of what she was shopping for, she said, but yes, she could see herself using this.

As Marta continued to poke around, Oliver whispered in my ear, "Thumbs-up on voice activation!" Marta hadn't called that feature out specifically, so I was surprised to hear Oliver felt it was a given, but perhaps I had missed it. I did not share Oliver's confidence that Marta would leverage voice activation; she had mentioned the importance of really understanding the materials behind her purchases as well as the craftsmanship, and voice-activated shopping would seem to undercut that process. At the risk of walking away with muddled information (and misleading Oliver), I needed to clarify exactly what she thought.

"It seems like it would be helpful to have a bit more visual detail to vet the garment you're considering," I said, reflecting back what I had heard.

"Yes," Marta said, "it's important to me that it's high quality."

"Great. What else?" I asked. Marta mentioned a few details she appreciated—being able to purchase directly in-app, for one, made shopping easier.

"The convenience of purchasing within the app is appealing to you," I said, once more reflecting back what I heard.

"Exactly," Marta confirmed.

"What else about this process feels convenient to you, if anything?" I asked. Convenience, the team thought, was the main appeal of including a feature like voice activation in the product, so when Marta teed the topic up, I had a clear path to dig deeper.

"Nothing really comes to mind," Marta said. "Maybe saving my credit card information—that helps. Although my credit card bill is usually twice as high when I do that." Ordinarily, I would not push further on the topic. Marta had not activated the feature herself during our walk-through, nor called out the feature as convenient or helpful. This suggested that she had seen the feature but not found it useful. I had given her ample opportunity to share her thoughts unprompted already. Though we try not to direct participants toward a feature, I needed one final checkpoint to confirm her perspective, or Oliver could leave with the wrong impression.

"I want to show you something now, and I wonder what you think of it. Take a look at this," I said, pointing to the voice-activation feature. "Did you notice that feature earlier?" I asked, playing dumb.

"Yes, that seems fine," Marta said, but that was too ambiguous for our purposes. Finally, I asked the question pointedly. "I want to make sure I'm getting this right. When you say it's fine, is it safe, then, to say you could see yourself using this?"

"Voice activation? Oh no," she said. It didn't take much more for Marta to share that actually, that feature just didn't feel necessary; she would never make a purchase without looking at it in detail first anyway, and besides, it felt weird to talk to her phone like that. Oliver was crestfallen, but at least we had the truth.

Two-Track Conversations

Two-track conversations occur when we think we and our conversation partner are talking about the same thing, but are actually not. If we aren't careful, we can spend entire conversations assuming we're on the same page when we're really miles apart.

This kind of misunderstanding can wreak havoc on our decision-making: A manager may give more independence to a direct report when what they really need is more hands-on support. An otherwise fair journalist may write an inaccurate article because they've misunderstood a source's position. A gift for a loved one may be a flop because we thought we knew—but were wrong about—what they really wanted. We may mistakenly end a conversation that is far from complete, and even inadvertently push each other away in the process.

Plus, being misunderstood just *feels bad*. If others consistently misread us, we might start to feel disappointed, or even ignored and disrespected. Feeling misunderstood may just be one of the loneliest emotions out there. Worse, in response to those feelings, we may feel pressured to up the ante on our position and defend it more forcefully (*She's not understanding me. This time I'll say it louder, and more explicitly.*). Or, we may decide that trying again to get our point across just isn't worth it and bail out entirely (*No way am I going to tell the instructor that wasn't what I was asking. I'll just have to google this tonight.*). When we raise our voices or abandon the conversation altogether, we are likely to leave more disconnected from our partner than when we started.

The best way to make sure you are picking up what your conversation partner is putting down is to vet and confirm your understanding. We can do this by making sense of what we've heard, playing back our understanding, observing reactions, and clarifying as needed to help us get past our manager's unwavering poker face, get through to our less than expressive partners, and follow the expert so technical her meaning is difficult to grasp.

Make Sense of What You Hear

To confirm our comprehension, we'll first need to untangle what's been said and make sense of it. Here, we must consider the context of our conversation, listen for signs that something important is being expressed, and observe body language, voice, and tone in real time to help us filter the right information. From there, we can identify key themes, begin to connect ideas, and uncover underlying emotions and meaning. We'll go into each of these steps next.

ESTABLISH CONTEXT

To make sense of what you are hearing, start by putting your conversation in context. The more information you have up front about what (and who) is important, the easier it is to listen for it in real time. Here are some points to be attentive to:

- **Scope and goals.** What is the purpose of this meeting, discussion, or conversation? Is it to come to a shared agreement about next steps, or is it to air our grievances? Is it to update and inform, or to call others to action? Answering this basic question for yourself can help you determine when a conversation goes off topic or stays on target, or when it is overly broad or far too narrow. Knowing what the conversation should look like makes it easier to filter out tangents, distractions, and interesting but ultimately out-of-scope musings.

- **Group dynamics.** Some voices are louder than others, but that does not mean they are the most influential. Especially in a group setting, whose opinion matters most? Who is the strongest influencer? Who is the ultimate decision-maker? And are they the same person? (Or, in more casual settings, who is so picky they are sure to cast the deciding vote on what restaurant we go to for dinner?) Understanding the roles of each member within the group can help you contextualize whether what's being said is need-to-know or nice-to-know information.

Knowing the context of a conversation up front gives you a map of what to expect and helps you to navigate what you are hearing.

MAP OUT KEY DETAILS to LOCATE WHAT'S IMPORTANT

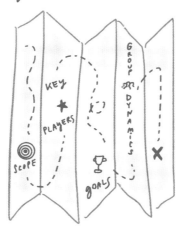

LISTEN FOR IMPORTANCE CUES

There are some verbal signals that can help us distinguish extraneous details from essential ones and tangents from main ideas. I call these *importance cues*. Importance cues are specific phrases that indicate we should listen up.

Some importance cues are more obvious than others. For instance, if a co-worker says, "Most importantly . . ." or a friend tells you, "The main issue is . . ." you can safely assume that you should pay attention to what comes next. Phrases like "Going back to your point," "To add to that," and "As I was saying earlier" can also signal importance: frequency or repetition of an idea are cues something pivotal is being said. The same idea expressed in multiple ways may also be an expression of importance.[1] Even stumbling can be a cue to listen for: we may trip on our words when an idea is still being fleshed out and requires more thought—and closer listening.

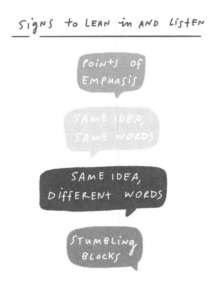

SCAN FOR BODY LANGUAGE, VOICE, AND TONE

Remember to pay attention to nonverbal signals to better understand what's been said. Observe for changes in posture, pitch, and emphasis. If your conversation partner says, "On top of *that* . . ." you know the stakes are being raised, and something important is coming.

IDENTIFY KEY THEMES

Simply parroting back what we've heard is not enough to make sense of what our conversation partner is saying; it is in the *process* of synthesizing their point of view that we begin to understand it.

To make meaning of all you've taken in, begin to group information into themes. On the next page are some phrases to listen for.

SYNTHESIZE WHAT YOU ARE HEARING

Phrase	Theme
• That changed everything . . . • That's when I realized . . .	Turning point or milestone
• Earlier I felt that . . . • I used to believe . . . • I now understand . . .	Progression
• Building off of what you said . . . • Adding to that . . .	Consensus
• If things were different, I would . . . • If I had it my way . . .	Compromise, yearning
• I'm not sure I agree that . . . • It's hard for me to see it that way given that . . . • The argument doesn't hold since . . .	Disagreement
• I can plan to . . . • Can you confirm you will . . . • It's decided that . . . • As a next step, let's . . .	Commitment

CONNECT IDEAS

As you start to synthesize the key themes of what your conversation partner is saying, look at how they might be connected. What does one thing (say, their frustration toward a particular project) have to do with the other (their team culture)? Could even seemingly disparate ideas (such as their productivity and the time of year) be connected? You can explore relationships between ideas using the frameworks below to focus and improve your understanding of what's been said:

- Time frame (days, weeks, months, years, seasons)
- Proximity (near and far)
- Causal (cause and effect)
- Correlative (related ideas)
- Systemic (order of operations)
- Emotional (passion, absence of)
- Resources (needed, available, unavailable)

LooK foR CoNNECtioNf BE+WEEN iᴅEAf to SEE the BiggER PictuRE

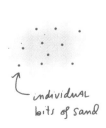

individuAL
bits of sand

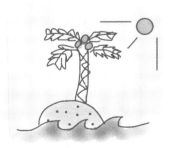

beach views

FOCUS ON THE HEART

In the end, however, the most important thing is to listen for how people feel. Focus on understanding underlying emotions above all, rather than sticking strictly to the literal. How does your conversation partner feel about what they are saying? Are they moved or staid? Calm or frantic?

WORDS   +   FEELINGS   =   MEANING

Listening for how people feel can help you understand, for instance, if a compromise is undertaken willingly, if a disagreement may have lasting effects on a relationship, or if consensus is forced or genuine.

As they emerge, underlying emotions might sound like:

- I'm having trouble with . . .
- I'm stuck on the fact that . . .
- It's hard for me to believe that . . .
- I feel like . . .

Play It Back

Once you have an initial understanding of what your conversation partner is saying, play it back to them for confirmation. To do this, summarize what you've heard, frame it neutrally and without bias, and use shared vocabulary.

GIVE A HEADLINE SUMMARY

Playing back what we have heard may sound easy enough in theory, but how do we know exactly what to highlight in the moment? Aim for a headline summary or bullet point recap—the TL;DR or executive summary version of what you've heard. Keep things short and sweet (e.g., a sentence) to make it easier for your conversation partner to quickly weigh in on whether you've gotten it right. Think like a beginner and use simple terms everyone can understand as you summarize to ensure terminology doesn't obscure the crux of the issue.

For example, instead of saying, "So, your manager is putting too much work on your plate, and you're doing a lot of projects at once this month," play it back, like, "It sounds like you're struggling to balance your workload." Or, rather than say, "Your roommate is emotionally needy and getting on your nerves, your sister won't stop calling, and your boss is a nightmare who turns to you for key projects but never gives credit where credit is due," give a high-level

recap and say, "It seems like you are in high demand—and under a lot of stress."

STAY NEUTRAL

There is a subtle but important difference between sharing your summary under the assumption that you've got it right and leaving the door open that you might have it wrong. For instance, chime in with "So what you're saying is . . ." and you may sound accusatory, or even bossy (*So what you're saying is you're tired of hanging out with me. Hmph!*). Ask instead, "What I'm hearing is . . . Does that sound right?" and you give your conversation partner permission to correct and clarify your thinking without ill will (*What I'm hearing is, you'd like some time to yourself. Is that right?*). This is also when you may choose to be strategic in your use of pronouns. "It sounds like we need more time to make a decision" has a far less adversarial connotation than saying, "It sounds like you're not ready to commit yet," for instance. However, be selective in your use of "we." Consistently saying "we" when you really mean "you" can sound hollow to others' ears.

Below are a few phrases you can use to play back what you've heard, and invite others to correct you as needed:

- It sounds like . . . is that a fair reading?

- You mentioned that . . . Did I get that right?

- Tell me if I've understood correctly . . .

- What I think I'm hearing is . . . Does that capture it?

- This seems important, and I want to make sure I'm getting it right . . .

USE EXISTING VOCABULARY

In research sessions, participants will frequently use their own words to describe a feature we, the internal team, are familiar with. Something we call a "feed" might be referred to as "the place where all my articles show up"; something we refer to as a "reaction" might be referred to as "the smileys, hearts, and thumbs-up icons underneath the article." Whether our participant gets the vocabulary right matters little to us (in fact, participants who know the technical terms for our features are often *too* advanced—too "techie" to be representative of the broader population). The important part is for participant and researcher to speak the same language.

When playing back what you've heard for confirmation, try not to introduce new vocabulary into the discussion but leverage shared vocabulary instead. This ensures you are as close as possible to speaking the same language as your conversation partner, which makes it easier for them to accept or reject your understanding of what they've said.

Using the same vocabulary as your partner also has the added benefit of equalizing parties in conversation. If you say "the small photos underneath the big photos that you swipe through" and I correct you and say the technical term is "carousel," you may not want to share your thoughts with me after that, much less correct me if I've misunderstood you. Similarly, if a friend shares that they are feeling the weight of the world on their shoulders, work with this metaphor to show you are listening rather than coming up with a new one, and definitely don't correct it.

CHECK YOUR BIASES

Abby VanMuijen is a Bay Area–based graphic recorder. During conferences and other events, she live-draws what she is hearing, creating large-scale visual summaries of speeches, workshops, classes, and the like. The job requires serious focus, fast hands, and an honest filter check to be successful.

Sometimes, Abby finds herself particularly passionate about a topic. "If it's something like politics, policy, or the future of education, I may have a view of what I would like the future of those to be like, and ideas I am hearing that I want to give voice to," she told me. Though she may prefer a particular idea to another, the visual summaries Abby creates must reflect how the ideas are received in real time—not according to her opinion, but according to that of the audience or workshop attendees. Especially when she covers events she is excited about, Abby knows she needs to check her biases before putting pen to paper.

"In those cases I have to keep an eye on myself to stay neutral," she said. "I have to be very cognizant of my own biases and my own internal agenda and filter for what I would like to see on the board. I have to do a lot of work both before walking into a room and also while I'm drawing. And then afterward, I look through and just have a real moment with myself of like, 'Did I blow up anything on here that *I* wanted to be bigger?'" If that turns out to be the case, Abby must revise her work, placing less emphasis on an idea that *she* was really excited about, but that was less enthusiastically received in the room.

In the same way, make sure that as you play back what you

have heard, you are doing so neutrally. Resist the urge to play back the bits *you* are most excited about (or even most upset about). Using the cues we looked at earlier, you can anchor on what is most important to the group or your conversation partner, not just what is most important to you. Ask yourself, as Abby does, "Did I blow up anything here that *I* wanted to be bigger?" If you did, dial it back in.

Read the Reaction

As you recap aloud what your conversation partner has said, gauge their reactions to help you assess if you are heading in the right direction.

"Can you tell me about what collaboration looks like on the team?" The candidate we were interviewing for a research role had a few minutes left of her interview, and, having aced her presentation, it was now her turn to ask the questions.

"I can speak to that," one of the designers piped in. "We observe research sessions, attend presentations, read the team's reports, and sometimes sit in on brainstorms they conduct." The candidate nodded and squinted.

For someone looking for a list of when, during an average research project, designers and researchers might interact, the designer's response would have been helpful. But when I looked at the candidate, she seemed dissatisfied and unsure of whether she should let the question go. She scribbled something in her notebook and stopped to look up as if to speak, before looking down again and scribbling some more. Though the designer had technically answered her question, I wondered if she had been looking for a more inspired response. She was a strong candidate, and I wanted us to have a strong finish, so I asked, "Does that answer your question?"

"Actually, I guess I'm wondering more about the day-to-day working styles of the team," she said. "Outside of the standard project milestones you mentioned earlier, what kind of partnership exists? And, this may sound silly, but do you socialize and have lunch together, or do the teams keep to themselves?"

"Ah!" the designer said, "I think I see what you mean." He was able to answer her question more completely after that.

We can use the observation skills we learned in chapter 3 to read our conversation partners' response as we play back their message. Their response can reveal how much we have correctly understood or mistakenly misheard. In particular, look for signs of:

- **Confusion.** Furrowed brows, blank stares, and squinting eyes can indicate that others are confused by your response. This may mean you misheard their earlier question or comment.

- **Disinterest.** Eyes glazing over, lack of eye contact, absent-mindedly examining hands, nail beds, and giving in to other distractions may indicate you've missed the point of what was said and are mistakenly responding in depth to a less than relevant detail.

- **Disappointment or frustration.** Should you mishear your conversation partner one too many times, you may observe disappointment or frustration, which can manifest as leaning back from the conversation, sighing, or even raised voices.

In addition, listen for sounds of:

- **Energy.** People are noisy when they are engaged. Mm-hmms, the sounds of others leaning in their seats, and scribbling notes become an orchestra of engagement.

- **Fidgeting.** Foot-tapping, pen-clicking, and other signs of fidgeting may signal impatience or lack of buy-in. (These can sound similar to nervousness, so be sure to use greater context clues to decode the situation accurately.)

- **Silence.** Silence is golden, except when it's in response to a conversation or discussion. Silence can signal disagreement, acquiescence, confusion, or any number of responses. Best to try again.

As you play things back, see how your conversation partner responds to your understanding of what they've said. Their reactions will make clear if you are on the right track or not.

Clarify

Sometimes the inputs we get—whether verbal or nonverbal, explicit or implicit—aren't enough to help us understand what our conversation partner means. When we're still uncertain, we have to gather more data to get it right. To do this, we can get feedback on our understanding, ask for clarity, and, when necessary, put it in writing.

GET FEEDBACK

If, as you play things back, you see confusion, disinterest, or other signals that indicate you may not have heard your conversation partner correctly, getting feedback, as I did with the job candidate, can help. The following questions can help you solidify your understanding and get back on track:

- Does that answer your question?
- Have I understood correctly?
- Is that what you were looking for?
- Does that seem like an accurate recap?

ASK FOR CLARITY

Sometimes we are really, truly in the dark on what our conversation partner means, and so unsure we do not know where to start. We may be in the presence of an expert and lack the vocabulary, context, and knowledge required to fully understand their position. We may be in the company of someone with a tremendous poker face, intentionally obscuring their position to their advantage (*Hello*, politicians, conference speakers, and media-trained celebrities!). Or we may simply be mentally foggy that day and need our conversation partner to be more explicit to ensure we are understanding correctly. In times when up can be down and down can be up, the only way out is through.

To escape from drowning in a sea of ambiguity, try the following phrases:

- What do you mean by that?
- I'm not sure I follow. I'm wondering if that means . . .
- I think I'm missing something. Can you break it down for me?
- Help me to understand your thinking. Do you mean that . . .
- Help me understand how you are feeling. Is it that . . .
- My understanding is . . . Please correct me if I'm wrong.

If asking for clarity seems intimidating (raise your hand if you don't particularly *like* asking for help), consider how much worse it is to be wrong in our understanding. Don't let a project go unstaffed because you don't understand the brief, or make an agreement or decision without fully understanding it. If you are truly blocked on your understanding, ask for clarity to help you move forward.

Be careful, however, not to overuse this approach. Use it too often, and your conversation partner may think you have a nervous tic, or, if they are less generous, that you are an idiot (*Why do I always have to break it down for him? How do things never click for her?*). Ask too early in the conversation, and your conversation partner may also think you are not a good listener (*I'm not finished yet!*).

Instead, try taking extra time up front to think through what's been said, considering what you know of your conversation partner given your personal history and conversation context, and using nonverbal signals to assess the situation; don't *start* here.

PUT IT IN WRITING

Recently, a friend of mine went on a work trip. After a full day of meetings and a festive team dinner, she happened to share a taxi back to the hotel with the head of the team, and they talked about how the day had gone.

"You know what would be great?" the director mused. "We should send a recap of the day to the VP when we're back at headquarters." My friend agreed—getting this kind of visibility could really help the team with future resources. "Maybe a one-pager," the director continued. "With input from you, Emilia, and Carmine."

"Totally agree," my friend said as they arrived at the hotel. "Great," said the director before waving goodbye. "See you tomorrow!"

As my friend got to her room, a wave of panic suddenly washed over her. She had *thought* the director was thinking aloud as she shared her idea. But upon further reflection, she began to doubt her initial instinct. What if she was actually asking *her* to write the one-pager? Should she be rounding up her co-workers to help? If the one-pager was for the vice president, it would have to be perfect, and they would have to get started first thing in the morning. On the other hand, if her director had simply been thinking aloud, taking action now could seem like she was overstepping. What to do? It was past midnight and far too late to clarify in person, so she had no choice: she had to reflect back her understanding over email.

Written communication is much harder to parse than in-person conversation, especially when you are not in the presence of the writer, so it is not my first recommendation for playing back what you have heard. Anyone who has ever written (or read) an email in haste knows how easy it is to misconstrue its meaning without the context of body language, facial expressions, and voice quality to offset the text on the page—end your email with "Thanks." instead of "Thanks!" and your message will read as completely different, even if your mood is unchanged. But if push comes to shove, a follow-up note may be the only way to confirm your comprehension. If we run out of time to play back what we've heard or have only limited access to our conversation partner, the written word can help.

If you go this route, keep things short and to the point: a simple "Recapping what I think I heard earlier, it sounds like . . ." will do.

In a note to her director, my friend outlined what she had heard and proposed next steps given their chat, adding, "Can you confirm if I've got it right?" That made it very easy for the director to quickly respond and reassure her that there was no formal ask behind their conversation, but that she had made a great sounding board. She could rest easy after that.

without confirming our comprehension,

we might BE Two SHips pAssing in the night

BEFORE YOU FORGET

On TV, misunderstandings are the stuff sitcoms are made of. But off-screen, the results are often far less humorous. When we misinterpret others or are misinterpreted ourselves, we begin to feel disconnected from each other and alone in our experience (*Why doesn't she get me?*). To avoid hurting others' feelings, becoming a punch line yourself, or making decisions under false assumptions, you'll want to confirm your comprehension of what your partner is saying in conversation.

CHAPTER 8

Guide the Conversation

There were ten minutes left in my research session, and I had a rambler on my hands. Jordana was polite, friendly, and chatty, but it was clear from the start that she had an agenda for our sixty-minute conversation together, and it didn't match mine. The session had so far been a grueling duel. I would ask a question, and she would give a surface-level response before pivoting to a topic irrelevant to my purposes. I would counter by returning to the original question and taking it a step deeper, and finally, she would respond with the texture and depth I needed—and then go off track yet again. I was exhausted as we neared the end of our session, but I still needed to learn a few more things.

"Let's talk about how you tell your business story. What's important for customers to know about your business?" I asked.

"I want them to know we are good quality and home grown," Jordana said. A great start, and I was curious to hear more. "Do you know who I would talk to about getting free ad credits?" As quickly as we had begun to make progress on the topic, she veered off course. It was clear that if I was going to get anything useful out of our conversation, I was going to have to redirect.

Redirecting is the quiet art of guiding your conversation partner toward or away from a conversation topic. It is helpful when your conversation partner is avoiding a subject, or getting stuck on a topic that has been well covered, and is especially helpful when you need the conversation to advance without ending it—such as in a meeting or at a dinner party, when abruptly leaving might be considered rude. Redirecting works by acknowledging where you are in conversation and politely nudging things along.

REDIRECTiNG hELPS guiDE thE CONVERSAtioN
to whERE it nEEDS to go

"To thE LEft!"   "To thE Right!"   "LowER now"

"HighER, pLEAſE"   "just a ſmiDgE mORE"   "PERfECt."

"I can definitely help with that," I told Jordana. "For now, I want to hit pause on that topic and really dig into understanding your business and your story. Your work is so interesting to me—let's come back to ad credits after."

"Sounds great," Jordana said, and we quickly got back to business.

Why did it work when I redirected Jordana? First, I made sure not to gloss over what she wanted but explicitly addressed it—by acknowledging her interest in ad credits, I let her know I was listening. Then I emphasized that I was genuinely intrigued by what she had to say. Finally, I reassured her that I was committed to getting her what she was looking for. This was a small but effective pivot, and the rest of our session went off without a hitch.

Redirecting serves two main purposes: it makes someone aware of where they are in conversation (whether they are spinning on a topic or going off track, dominating the conversation or about to put their foot in their mouth), and it protects both your and your conversation partner's time and energy.

When we fail to redirect—because we don't know how or prefer not to—everyone in the conversation suffers. We may be exposed to an awkwardly personal spat that we are deeply uncomfortable witnessing, or we may resent a colleague using up precious meeting time that would otherwise be more equitably distributed. We may even begin to feel unsafe and in need of protection if others' interest in us has begun to feel invasive and ill-intentioned. In moments like these, redirecting is a helpful tool to get us through. We'll look at how to keep conversations on course in these scenarios, and more, next.

Redirect to Combat Avoidance

Gabriela had told me in advance that she had an update for me. Generally when a direct report asks for a last-minute meeting and wants to provide an "update," it's a pretty safe bet they are about to resign. I felt a sinking feeling in my stomach, as I always do when these invitations pop up on my calendar; no matter how many times you deal with a resignation, it's never fun. Still, I'd been through enough of these conversations to know that they are necessary, to appreciate that career paths are full of twists and turns, and to understand that change is normal, and welcome.

Gabriela and I met in the company café, where we usually go for one-on-ones, and exchanged the usual chitchat and weekend updates. Afterward, Gabriela launched in: "I was thinking when we run our next workshop, it would be good to include more of the engineering team. I think they'll really benefit from being exposed to more user stories to help build empathy." Not where I thought she'd start, but yes, that sounded like a good approach. "Also, my current project is going well; my team is in the loop and I'm planning a brainstorm for later this week to explore some new design concepts and future product features." OK, that sounded good to me, too, but my Spidey sense was telling me this wasn't *really* the point of this meeting. "And the report I'm working on is almost ready for your feedback. Can I send that to you tomorrow?"

We were halfway through our allotted time, but it seemed to me that we were far from where Gabriela wanted to be: she was talking at a rapid clip, shifting in her seat more than usual, and seemed to be gearing herself up for something.

"Yes, of course," I said, "but I want to do a quick time check since I know there was a specific update you were hoping to share. We've got about fifteen more minutes, just as a heads-up."

"Right," Gabriela said, "I plan to do everything we just talked about, and also, I wanted to give you my two weeks' notice." There it was!

Sometimes our conversation partner has something important to share, but for one reason or another (fear, shame, guilt, nerves) might avoid sharing it. When we know our partner has something to say—because they have told us as much, or because their current behavior or even body language suggests as much—we can steer the conversation to where they've indicated they would like it to go.

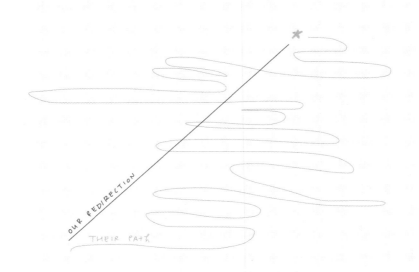

There are two simple but effective techniques to employ when your conversation partner is avoiding the topic at hand.

GIVE A REMINDER

A reminder can embolden others to drive the conversation they may have been hoping for. At the same time, a reminder shows them that you are tracking their intention and are ready to receive what they have to say. Knowing that you are both on the same page can serve as a small encouragement toward sharing what they actually want to address in conversation.

Here are a few phrases you can use to coax your conversation partner toward what's really on their mind:

- You mentioned you wanted to talk about . . .

- I know you've been thinking about . . . Should we talk about that now?

- There was something else you wanted to discuss . . .

- I'm remembering there's something in particular you wanted to cover. Should we tackle that?

APPLY PRESSURE

Applying a small amount of pressure can also create the necessary urgency to address things head-on. In my conversation with Gabriela, I hoped that by surfacing our remaining time together, this might encourage her to address what was on her mind. Simply reminding your conversation partner of how much time you have left together (or how much time you've spent on a possibly irrelevant topic) can be enough to help them see where they need to direct their attention. Try, for instance:

- It's getting late; should we chat about . . . ?

- The [café closes, train arrives, meeting ends] in thirty minutes; let's cover . . . first.

- I want to be mindful of your time; let's talk through . . . now.

- We're halfway through our time together—should we prioritize talking about . . . ?

Redirect to Stop Spinning

A friend of mine is in training to be a career coach. One of her clients was a young thirtysomething and recent MBA graduate in a professional rut. He didn't know what he wanted to do next and had a hefty student loan bill to contend with.

"I'm thinking of going into recruitment, or maybe HR, or possibly management, or potentially marketing," he said. OK, my friend thought, that's a lot, but it's a start. "But I don't know, I'm not really finding anything I like, no matter how hard I look. There's just nothing out there for me," her client sighed. As quickly as he had ramped up his exploration, he had gotten discouraged.

"What's interesting to you about those roles?" my friend asked, employing a connecting question to try to find the common thread or driving interest that tied them all together.

"I'm pretty sure I could get hired for these positions," he said. It was hardly an inspired answer, so my friend dug deeper.

"So these are jobs we think you could confidently get," she said, using an expansion prompt.

"Yes, I think my background would be a match," he said, pausing as a flicker of concern crossed his face. "If I can't get *these* jobs, I don't know what I'll do . . . What if there's nothing out there for me? Maybe you could introduce me to some of your professional contacts in those fields?"

Sometimes our conversation partner is spinning and needs an assist to home in on the issue at hand. The most common signals that someone is stuck in conversation are:

- **Fixation.** Circling on the same path, focusing exclusively on a single idea or feeling—such as the inaccessibility of the job market

- **Hopelessness.** Seeing no way out of a given situation; a glass-half-empty point of view

- **Repetitive language.** Using the same language time and time again to express one's fixation, not straying from one's initial talking points

When others circle around the same set of ideas throughout a conversation without progressing, we may need to redirect them to more fruitful territory. The following strategies can help you do this.

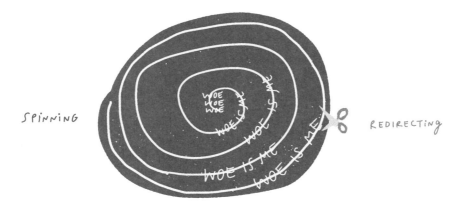

HELP OTHERS SEE THAT THEY ARE STUCK

Sometimes redirecting is as simple as raising awareness that someone is stuck, so that together you can move forward on a topic, instead of circling around it. When you redirect, hold up a mirror for your conversation partner and help them see where they may be stuck. Be honest and provide a gentle reality check if it's needed.

Knowing her client was spinning, my friend redirected by carefully articulating something he likely already knew (but may have needed to hear from someone else): "I'm happy to help make an intro when you're ready," she said gently, "but it sounds like you might need more time to think about what you really want before throwing your hat in the ring." In the end, he agreed.

The phrases below can be used to redirect the conversation and help your partner see their problem spot:

- It seems like this is important to keep thinking through.
- It sounds like it might help to dig in here.

- I get the sense you are still working on this.
- It feels like this might need more thought.
- I want to go back to something you said earlier.
- You mentioned something that really stuck with me.

REFRAME THE SITUATION

Sometimes our conversation partner is stuck because they can only see the problem in one way. When their perspective is fixed, a change in framing can help them make progress. For instance, if our conversation partner's perspective is anchored in the future, pointing them toward the present can reboot their thinking (*We know where you want to be; what can we do about this today?*). For those who are stuck in the past, jumping ahead to the future may help them make progress (*We know what the constraints are today. What if we picture the future?*). Similarly, steering our conversation partner to consider different points of reference may help them go from treading water to swimming in a new direction (*What would you do if money were no object? What would you do if you had all the time in the world?*).

Use the following phrases to reframe the situation and encourage a fresh perspective in conversation:

- What happens if we think about it from this angle?
- What if we assume the reverse to be true?
- What if we take this as a given?
- What if we assume that's up for grabs?

- What if we imagine all options are on the table?
- What if we change our time frame?

Redirect to Include Others

Not long ago, I was gathering input from my team on how well they felt we were collaborating with our design counterparts. I had a clear perspective on this, namely, that we weren't partnering much at all—not out of malice but out of lack of intentionality, for which I was partly responsible. But did my team feel the same way?

One of my more tenured directs, Colette, kicked us off, as she often does; she is never shy to tell you how she feels. "The design team doesn't get much respect from Engineering, if you ask me. It seems like they only care about fostering that relationship right now," she said. "They don't even show up to our share-outs anymore." Thus began a thorough account of Colette's interactions with the design team and how they were falling short.

As Colette continued, I could see her teammates begin to lose focus. Laptops that were once closed now sprang open, Slack messages flew, and attention waned. Though her input was essential, the more time went by, the less space there seemed to be for the others. To get a comprehensive look at the problem, I would have to redirect.

"Thank you, Colette, for getting us started and for refreshing our memory on some of our work with the design team," I said before opening it up to the group. "It sounds like Colette's experience with Design has been somewhat strained. Paulo," I said, turning to another member of the team, "What has your experience been like?"

Sometimes you need to redirect to make sure everyone's voice is heard. Especially in group discussions, where personalities and conversation styles vary, it may be helpful to facilitate the conversation in a way that encourages participation.

TRACK AIRTIME

A good starting point for this is to track conversation *airtime*, or the active speaking time each participant is getting. Airtime includes every interruption, question posed, speech given, or verbal contribution to the group—which for some can add up to a lot, and for others to almost nothing at all.

Sometimes, the group's dynamics are obvious, even predictable. One member of the group may dominate others, like Colette, who was always ready to lead the charge in conversation. Others may have thoughtful opinions that emerge when they are explicitly invited to participate, like Paulo, who I knew from experience would weigh in only when asked.

In other cases, you may not be intimately familiar with the group's dynamics—they may instead reveal themselves to you in real time. For instance, when researchers run a workshop, they invite a group of participants to share their thoughts on a topic in a group setting. We cannot predict who will be chattiest and who will be quietest among the group, but we *can* predict that there will be a range of conversation styles, which may necessitate redirecting. Especially in discussions where group dynamics are unknown, you can track how much airtime each participant is getting, and keep an ear out for when someone dominates the conversation. When discussions are off balance, redirecting can help you establish equal footing among the group. If everyone gets a chance to opine, the discussion will be much richer.

PASS THE MIC

In discussion with the group, it turned out Colette was not the only one feeling disconnected from the design team, but she was the only one who felt the engineering team had exacerbated the problem. Passing the mic to others helped bring the broader team in to more accurately pinpoint the source of tension in the partnership (in our case, lack of role clarity) and what we could do about it.

The following redirecting phrases can bring equilibrium to the group. These work by acknowledging one party's input before inviting others to contribute—this way no one feels dismissed or ignored, and everyone feels heard.

- Thank you for that detail and context. What else do people think?

- I appreciate the input. How does that resonate with everyone else?

- Recapping X's experience, it sounds like . . . What are others' experiences like?

- That's a [fair point, good idea, reasonable request, etc.]. Thoughts from the other side of the table?

- Thank you for sharing how you feel. Let's bring the rest of the group in now.

Redirect to Get Back on Track

My team and I were having lunch to celebrate a colleague's promotion. Ines, a member of the team, was recounting at length a story about a disastrous attempt to book flight arrangements through a third-party website. There had been an initial reservation and then a need to change it, a phone call to the airline and another to the third-party operator, a check-in for the wrong flight and a snafu on the refund, and more from there. I will spare you the gory details, but suffice to say that it is *always* best to book a flight directly through their proprietary website if you think you'll need the flexibility to make changes to your booking (sorry, Orbitz).

As Ines told her story in painstaking detail, my mind began to wander. I looked at my colleagues, and it was clear theirs had begun to do the same: a co-worker who is usually wide-eyed and encouraging in conversation looked strained and tired. Another studiously perused the menu as if it were the most fascinating item in the world. Still another began to absentmindedly examine her cuticles, providing the occasional mm-hmm to demonstrate she was still (sort of) with us. One co-worker attempted to interject and move things along, but Ines was so passionate about telling her story that the interruption was rebuffed (*I'm not finished yet!*). And then there was poor Elsa, the guest of honor, politely listening to Ines when we should have been celebrating her and sending her off in style. This would be a frustrating meal if one of us didn't find a path forward.

To politely steal the mic from Ines, I said, "Ines, I'm afraid I'm going to have to stop you there. We've got Elsa to celebrate on her big day, and I know her manager wants to say a few words before we order." Passing it off to Elsa's manager did the trick without making anyone feel bad. The table perked up—Ines, too.

PROTECT THE AGENDA

If you have one, reiterating the agenda at hand is a simple and straightforward way to keep conversations from getting derailed. These phrases help you return to the relevant topic of discussion if a member of the group is running away with it. They work especially well in more formal settings, like the office. The next time you find yourself working hard to keep the conversation from wandering, try these on for size.

- Let's concentrate on what we were talking about earlier.
- How about we return to the goal at hand?

- Let's remember what we wanted to discuss.

- Why don't we come back to that?

Outside the office, many of our conversations come with agendas, even if we don't call them that, as we saw in chapter 6. For instance, if you're catching up with an old friend and are overdue for a life update, the "agenda" may be to jam a year's worth of milestones into one dinner. If the conversation strays and your friend starts to recount everyone's personal news but her own, and you're eager to hear how she's been, you can reiterate the "agenda" to get back on track with a few well-placed phrases:

- Catch me up on that [new promotion, engagement story, work milestone, etc.].

- Remind me about [how you're settling into that new job, what the latest is on the home front, etc.].

- Let's go back to that [life update] you were going to share.

- Talk to me about [how you've been feeling, how the family is, etc.].

MANAGE TANGENTS

Some people are repeat offenders when it comes to taking us off target in conversation. When this happens, it's best to address them directly about their behavior, whether they are aware of this habit or not. For best results, pair your observation with a request to understand.

For instance:

- I've noticed you've had a tendency to take us off topic today. Is there something you'd like to share with me?
- You've diverted us a few times already. Is there something that's bothering you?
- It seems your mind is elsewhere today. Should we talk about that?

In some cases, following up in the moment will be your best bet to getting things back on track. However, if you suspect there's something personal going on for your conversation partner, waiting till the group has dispersed may be appropriate, lest your partner feel forced to share more than they are comfortable with before a larger audience.

Redirect to Change the Pace

Not every conversation topic requires the same amount of time and attention. Sometimes we need to speed things up to get to the point or uncover our conversation partner's core needs. Other times we may need to slow things down and spend more time on a given topic, even if our conversation partner is avoiding it.

Without an agenda, how do we know when we are spending too much—or too little—time and attention on a given topic? When you are considering redirecting to change a conversation's pace, ask yourself these questions:

- Does this topic merit five minutes or fifty?

- Are we making progress by tackling this quickly?

- Could we make more progress by tackling this slowly?

- Is more space needed to get to the heart of things or has too much been given already?

- Do I need more time to understand the issue?

WhEN the CoNVeRSAtioN is stuck oR headiNg in the wRoNg DiREctioN, ChANgE the pacE to get BACK ON tRACK

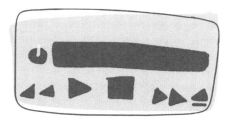

When you have determined that a topic is worthy of more discussion, or, on the contrary, that we've said all we need to say, the following phrases can help. They work by being explicit about our intent and our proposed direction.

These phrases create space to delve deeper into a topic:

- I think it's worth spending more time here.

- I want to go back to something you said earlier.

- You mentioned something that piqued my interest.

- Let's give this some more thought.

These phrases keep things moving along:

- I want to switch gears for a minute . . .

- I'm also hoping to talk about . . .

- Let's make sure we also cover . . .

- I want to make sure we get to catch up on . . .

Redirect to Avoid Faux Pas

We've all made our share of missteps in conversation before, some big and some small. Perhaps we forgot someone's name—or worse, called them the wrong name—despite having met them multiple times. Maybe we accidentally asked invasive questions about someone's personal life, like whether they are married, want children, or make a good living, when we didn't actually have permission to go there. We may have told a joke that didn't land well, talked about ourselves for too long, or even let a swear or two slip at the office. Some of us have even mistakenly congratulated a woman for her pregnancy when she was not actually pregnant. The list of possible faux pas is long.

When we commit a faux pas, we are often mortified by our behavior (*I can't believe I assumed she was pregnant!*), ashamed (*I probably shouldn't swear in front of my co-workers, especially as their manager.*), or even feel guilty (*This person always remembers my name; why can't I do the same for them?*). We may also feel we should

have known better. We often wish we hadn't said anything at all—
or that our conversation partner could have stopped us before we
went too far (*I really stepped in it this time, and he watched me like a
train wreck in slow motion.*).

As listeners, we can help prevent the embarrassment and discomfort such moments bring. When your conversation partner is
on the verge of committing a faux pas or building themselves a bad
reputation, you can helpfully steer the conversation to more neutral
ground. In these cases, redirecting may sound less pointed, since
there is a benefit to being discrete.

INTRODUCE A NEW TOPIC

Introducing a new topic is a gentle way to shift attention away
from a potentially dangerous subject and to one everyone can
safely enjoy. To do this, you can use *transition phrases*: tiny pivots
that help us to go into new territory in conversation. Try, for instance:

- I was hoping we could think through . . .
- I also wanted to talk about . . .
- I've been meaning to catch you up on . . .
- Let's make sure we cover . . .

USE EMERGENCY PIVOTS

Emergency pivots are a last-ditch effort to steer the discussion to a
safe and neutral zone that may have little to do with the conversation at hand. Because they require jumping in at a moment's notice,

they may sound less polite than transition phrases. They can be jarring but effective when the situation is dire.

Emergency pivots sound like non sequiturs and can include just about anything you can think of that will be safer territory than the current topic. For instance:

- Have you seen the latest on . . . ?
- Did you hear the news about . . . ?
- I'm excited to [see a new show, take a vacation, try the pasta, etc.]!
- How about them Yankees?

HIT PAUSE

Sometimes we don't have a new topic of discussion on the tip of our tongue, but we do know we need to stop the conversation in its tracks. If you can see an accident waiting to happen and can't think of what to say to move the conversation to more neutral ground, simply focus on hitting pause. In the face of a looming faux pas, keeping things short and sweet may be the best option. For instance:

- Let's come back to that.
- Hold that thought.
- Hang tight for a second.
- Let's table that for now.

PROVIDE AN ESCAPE ROUTE

If your attempts to change the subject or hit pause have failed, it might be time to hit eject. For the sake of you and your conversation partners, you may need to redirect by pulling someone out of a conversation entirely. You can politely tap a friend out of rotation (*Mind helping me in the kitchen? I could use an extra set of hands right now.*) or pull a co-worker from a meeting (*Can I borrow you for a minute?*).

Redirect to Mediate Disputes

A family dinner was well underway, and what a feat it was to have twenty-two seats filled with warm and loving faces. Everyone had come in from far-flung places to spend the holidays together and meet the new grandchildren, nieces, and nephews. Glasses clinked in celebration, and compliments went to the chef. The mood was festive—until two of the siblings started bickering over parenting styles (*You can't let an infant cry it out. That's terrible! I would never . . . Yes, and that's why your child is such a poor sleeper! Good luck sleeping through the night with that attitude. My child . . .*). And so on.

Opinions on sleep training will vary no matter the family—that was not the problem. The problem was that, without realizing it, the siblings' voices had begun to rise. Their argument quickly carried across the table, and what had begun as a minor disagreement in one corner was now a major public display of sibling infighting. The group was used to seeing the pair squabble, but this was too much. It was the holidays, and everyone had flown from so far to be here—couldn't we all just get along? Someone needed to manage the situation and redirect the conversation: to ease the group's discomfort and help the siblings see that their arguing had gone too far. But when no one jumped in, the two kept at it and the argument escalated, eventually ending with a slammed door and an awkward silence. The night now seemed ruined.

Sometimes we need to deescalate a conversation that's getting out of control. With kind but firm redirecting, we can guide the conversation to smoother terrain.

MAKE A DEAL

In the heat of the moment, our conversation partners may not be ready to walk away from their quarrel. When a dispute is on the verge of becoming an all-out brawl, we can use the promise of future resolution to redirect. Each of the phrases below acknowledges our interlocutors' tender spot and gently steers the conversation toward new ground, with a suggestion to return to the subject as needed:

- I understand you feel strongly about this subject. Since not everyone here can relate, maybe we can return to this with a smaller crowd later. Would that be OK?

- I can see you have a lot to say on the topic. If it's all right with you, let's come back to this after we finish [celebrating, toasting, etc.].

- Your passion for [sleep training, etc.] is palpable, but perhaps we can continue that discussion after dinner. Are you open to that?

WE CAN MEDIATE to fiND A wAy foRWARD

WELCOME DETOUR

ARGUE

INSULT

TAKE A

REP BOTH SIDES

You can also defuse an argument by focusing on the underlying emotions of the dispute. Summarize what you are hearing and reflect back feelings to help everyone understand the real causes of friction. You'll likely recognize this technique if you've been to couples or family therapy, or if you've ever had to negotiate a situation between two young children (*Sophie's feelings were hurt, and you were angry.*).

Consider the following phrases:

- It sounds like you are experiencing it in this way . . . , and she is experiencing it in that way . . .
- It looks like one side feels . . . , and the other feels . . .
- He is . . . and she is . . .

If you find yourself trying to resolve a dispute *you* are a part of, the same rules apply: focus on voicing the underlying emotions you've understood from your conversation partner and be careful to stay neutral and reserve judgment. The point is not to say "*You* are being sensitive and I am just joking" but to say "I can see that your feelings are hurt and that I am part of why you feel that way." It's harder to be mad at someone when you're taking in their feelings.

It's a good idea to also share your own feelings, and to let your conversation partner in on what you are experiencing. "I am feeling insecure about the topic" or "This subject brings up a lot of anxiety for me" helps illustrate the full picture. Exploring these feelings together can help you resolve your dispute.

Whether you are repping someone else's feelings or your own, take care not to explain *why* you are each behaving the way that you are—at least not to start—since it is very easy to blame others for our feelings if we aren't careful. "I'm feeling insecure about the topic" can quickly turn into "I'm feeling insecure about the topic because you are always trumpeting your successes," and "This subject brings up a lot of anxiety for me" can swiftly become "This subject brings up a lot of anxiety for me because you put so much pressure on me to be perfect."

The goal is to get to a place where we can say, "When X happened, it made me feel Y, even though I now understand you didn't mean it that way." When emotions are clarified, quibblers tend to soften and understand, if not resolve.

SHUT IT DOWN

Of course, depending on the relationship, your approach to resolution might be much more blunt: "Ladies, you're both wonderful parents no matter how you sleep train. Let's get back to celebrating!" Or even "Knock it off, you two. Let's move on." When a promise to defer the topic until later is too gentle for the group (or even impossible), shutting it down and moving on may do. We'll talk more about this technique in chapter 9.

Redirect to Protect Yourself

There is a co-worker with whom I always say too much. Over the years I've learned she's not the most trustworthy of peers, and yet, even though I start our one-on-ones with my guard up, by the end of our conversation she's managed to pull something out of me that I never intended to share. I consider myself a fairly level-headed person, but I acknowledge that this behavior is by no means rational. Time and again I've stopped to reflect after one of these encounters on just what went wrong. Did I temporarily forget about her untrustworthiness? I know that can't be right when I mentally prepare myself before meeting her. Hypnotized? Not likely. And yet.

The last time we caught up, it hit me: she was using a research moderating skill on me—one that we learned about earlier in chapter 6, and that comes in handy when you sense others have more to say. She was, quite simply (but very subtly), using silence to wait me out. Though I was intimately familiar with the tactic, I had completely missed that she was employing it on me.

I suspect that this co-worker knew what she was doing, and I felt slightly manipulated when I put two and two together. Given this revelation, if it were up to me, our paths would not cross again. But unless I quit, that wasn't going to be possible.

Now when I have a meeting with her, I take a different approach. I no longer fill the silence when she waits me out, nor do I answer personal questions about my career aspirations or share professional gripes. I can still have a cordial conversation with her, but I'm not giving intel up so easily. So when she tees me up with a "Isn't this reorg really something? I guess this puts a lot of teams up for grabs. Interesting, isn't it?" I no longer take the bait and admit that yes, the politics of this organizational change are the stuff of soap operas, and yes, I am interested in expanding my scope to include one of the many teams that will soon be rudderless and at bay. Instead, I redirect, and say, "It's something all right. Now about that project that's due soon . . ."

DEFLECT

When you need to redirect a conversation to protect yourself from your conversation partner's ill intent, you can do so without laying all your cards on the table. This can be particularly helpful in situations that call for you to play nice, be diplomatic, or conceal that you are aware of the other person's intention (and how you feel about it). Think: office politics, delicate conversations with in-laws, and other fraught relationships that may not be able to withstand honesty.

The following redirecting phrases can be used without revealing your motivation:

- That reminds me of . . .
- How interesting. In other news . . .

- Speaking of . . . Have you heard about . . . ?
- I've been meaning to update you on . . .

STAND YOUR GROUND

In some cases, it may be necessary to be explicit about why you are redirecting. If we are comfortable with our conversation partner or if we do not fear reprimand, it can be more productive to let them know why we are redirecting, especially if our conversation partner has crossed a moral or ethical line, or overstepped a boundary.

Try, for instance:

- I'm not comfortable with where this conversation is going. Let's look at . . . instead.
- This conversation is getting out of hand, and I feel compelled to step in. I recommend we shift to . . . instead.
- This is totally unprofessional and uncalled for. A better subject would be . . .
- It seems like we are getting ourselves unnecessarily riled up. Why don't we talk about . . . instead.

Beware the Savior Effect

I once had a conversation with a junior researcher who felt dismissed after a senior colleague redirected him during a team meeting. We were having a "meet and greet" with a newly hired director. The junior researcher asked her some tough questions about her leadership experience. "I heard you've never managed a research team before," he asked. "Are you ready to lead us as part of your new team?"

The director took his question seriously and paused to consider it before giving a thoughtful and honest response. The junior researcher had a follow-up, he said, if that was OK. But before the director could respond, a senior member of the team jumped in. "Actually, on a lighter note, what are some of your hobbies?"

This particular senior colleague tends to play a nurturing role on the team, so she may have thought she was saving the director from an uncomfortable question. But the effect was jarring: nervous laughter filled the room and the director obliged with a list of activities she enjoyed. Later, the junior researcher confided in me that he felt both misunderstood and disrespected by the senior colleague's redirection (*What's wrong with asking honest questions of our leaders?*). Later on, the director thanked the junior researcher for asking the hard questions.

When you find yourself compelled to redirect on behalf of others, ask yourself: Do I have all the necessary information, or might I be jumping to conclusions about what is happening here? What the senior colleague didn't know is that the junior employee had cleared his questions with his manager, who encouraged him to put them forth to the director, his new boss.

It also pays to self-reflect on your instinct to "save" your conversation partner, and to interrogate your honest motivation. Consider: Do I want to redirect because my conversation partner is truly uncomfortable, or to ease my own discomfort? If it's the latter, do your best to tolerate your discomfort. If the discomfort turns to danger, of course, redirect or exit as you wish. (We'll talk about how to effectively exit a conversation in the following chapter.)

And remember, you may not be the only concerned listener in the group. It may not be "on you" to redirect every time. Trust others to do this, too—especially if they are more central to the conversation.

EXERCISE: Practice Redirecting

Consider the scenarios below and sketch out how you might redirect.

- Your teammates are brainstorming solutions for a thorny problem and the team lead is dominating the discussion. What could you say to ensure every voice is heard?

- A friend is bemoaning the state of her dating life, playing the same breakup story over and over again. What could you say to move things along?

- You'd like your parents' blessing on your new relationship, but when you raise the topic, they dodge it. How might you get to the heart of things?

- A co-worker is fishing for information from you. What could you say to protect yourself from her inquiry?

- Your roommates are bickering, and it's getting personal. How might you steer things to more neutral terrain?

BEFORE YOU FORGET

When you can tell that a conversation has become unproductive or unsafe, you can tactfully employ redirecting phrases to guide it in the right direction. Having these phrases in our tool kit helps us stay active and engaged instead of tuning out or sitting back when our conversation partner needs us most.

CHAPTER 9

Make an Exit

On paper, Larry was the perfect participant. My team and I were conducting a study on young professionals and their career aspirations, and he had ticked off all the right answers in our screener, a short set of questions meant to help us weed out anyone who might not match the profile of participants we hoped to talk to. Larry fit the demographic we were interested in learning from, had grand career aspirations, and had even used our platform during a job search before. Plus, he was from Illinois, and we had deliberately looked to counterbalance tech-centric Bay Area views with those of the broader country. Larry was a shoo-in.

But from the start of our call, things were rocky. Although we had triple-confirmed with participants that they would have strong Wi-Fi and a stable internet connection, Larry's video call dropped over and over again. We tried turning off video, but the connection was still faulty. Then, Larry's laptop ran out of juice, so he dialed in from his phone—which would be a problem later in the call, since we wanted to show him a clickable prototype of a website—not something he could easily test from a handheld device.

The technical difficulties were bad enough, but any researcher who has run a remote study before knows these hiccups come with the territory. But even when the connection *was* clear, we realized we still had a problem. The more questions I asked Larry, the more it seemed like he was not the right person to talk to.

"Tell me what a typical visit to our site looks like for you," I asked Larry.

"I love that I can post pictures and share them with my network," Larry said—which was an odd thing to say, because the website currently didn't have the functionality to post photos.

"When you say pictures, what kinds of pictures do you mean?" I asked, just to be certain that I wasn't misunderstanding him—participants often use their own vocabulary in sessions, and it's the researcher's job to understand their meaning.

"Oh, all kinds of pictures!" he said eagerly. His ambiguous reply left me wanting, so I offered some specifics for him to react to.

"Do you mean photos, or more like articles, emoji, something else entirely?"

"Oh, yes, all of that. Photos, articles, and emoji. Yes, it's such a wonderful thing," he said. But this didn't make any sense, either.

I turned to the homework exercise I had sent the night before. "Homework" refers to any assignment a researcher sends to their participant in advance; it gives the researcher additional data and a starting point from which to dive into a topic, and gets the participant in the right state of mind for the conversation. In this case, I had asked Larry to gather images that represented his feelings about his job.

"OK," I said, pivoting. "Let's talk through your homework. Why don't you show me what you came up with."

"Oh, that email?" said Larry. "Yeah I didn't have a chance to do it." This was not ideal. Of course, as with children, you cannot guarantee a participant will do their homework, but you hope they will.

"No problem," I said, forging ahead. "Let's talk through it now." I continued, vetting his answers as I went, until it became clear that Larry was, well, lying.

Sometimes in research studies, you get a bad recruit. People may intentionally lie on their screeners because they want to make a quick $100, or accidentally misrepresent themselves if they misunderstand your question or answer it absentmindedly. I would not know until after the session which bucket Larry fell into, but in the moment, I knew we had to end the conversation. The more we pressed on, the clearer it became that Larry had no idea what we were talking about.

In the beginning of my career, I might have tried to make it work—to see if I could learn something relevant for the team, even if Larry wasn't exactly our target user. But experience has taught me that the juice is not worth the squeeze—you wind up with data you can't use, and you eat into your team's time, as well as your own and the participant's. Why slog through a bad fit? In these cases, it's not enough to redirect the conversation—it's better to just cut and run.

So twenty minutes into our sixty-minute call, I said, "Larry, thank you so much for your time today. I've learned so much from you already, and I don't want to keep you any longer than neces-sary," I said.

Larry was delighted by this turn of events. "Oh wow, that's great! And I'll still get paid?" I assured him his check would arrive within the week, and thanked him once again. When the call ended, the team sighed in relief. We would find someone else.

Sometimes redirecting is not enough, and we need to end a conversation entirely and make an exit. In the lab, we may end a session if our participant isn't a good fit, or if we have all the infor-mation we need from them. In real life, the circumstances for end-ing a conversation look different: we may feel overwhelmed to the point where a time-out will no longer suffice. If a conversation be-comes dangerous or toxic, we may need to get out of Dodge. Or, we may simply have conflicting priorities we must attend to. Unlike redirecting, which helps us change course but stay in conversation, ending the conversation means exiting it entirely.

When we don't draw the line, our relationships suffer. Call me one too many times to vent about your partner without ever checking in on me, and I may begin to resent that you've designated me as your couple's counselor. Sense you are in danger of being manipulated by a "friend" one too many times, and you may find yourself declining future social invitations. If meetings with a co-worker repeatedly run over and cause you to miss your train home, you may start to dread working with them and wonder if you can be reassigned to a different project. If we never learn to exit the conversation, we tire ourselves out, our trust in each other erodes, and we begin to feel hurt and alone. At the risk of becoming a *listening martyr*—someone who goes into conversations so focused on the other person that they lose themselves entirely—we need to find our way out of conversations that do us harm and into those that recharge our spirit.

Luckily, there are ways to end these conversations before they leave us emotionally burdened, make us feel unsafe, or just cause us to be late to our next engagement. Closing the conversation should be done sparingly, lest our conversation partners think us evasive, overly emotional, or even unreliable, but when it's called for you'll be glad you have these tactics at your disposal. At the same time, if you find yourself consistently deploying this technique with the same person time and again, that may be a sign that the relationship has larger deficits to address.

To effectively end a conversation, there are several techniques to master. We'll look at these next.

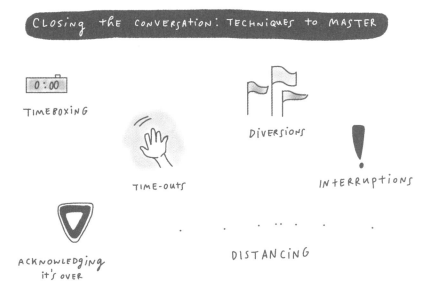

CLOSING the CONVERSATION: TECHNIQUES to MASTER

0:00 TIMEBOXING

TIME-outs

DIVERSIONS

INTERRUPTIONS

ACKNOWLEDGing it's over

DISTANCING

Timebox the Conversation

In a research session, the time we spend together with a participant is highly structured, even if it doesn't feel that way to them. From the outside, a good session looks and sounds like an ordinary conversation—it ebbs and flows and "happens" to cover a lot of ground in a short period of time. But behind the scenes, researchers have carefully crafted guides with a set amount of time they intend to spend on any number of topics. We may budget a few minutes up front for establishing rapport, reserve a quarter of an hour to more deeply understand a participant's needs or motivations, and save the bulk of our time for going through a workflow, walking through a typical visit to a website, or evaluating a prototype, before wrapping up with summary questions.

In our day-to-day, the reasons for budgeting our time in this way may look different, but the winning technique is the same. *Timeboxing* means giving our conversation partner a set amount of time before we move on from a conversation. We may employ this technique when we are ill-equipped to give the empathy our partner deserves—because we are tired, distracted, or even emotionally activated—or when we need to draw a line and protect ourselves from being taken advantage of.

Timeboxing works particularly well when we are listening to those who require more from us than we can give, but whom we may be incentivized to keep happy—the co-workers we must play nicely with, the neighbors we'd be wise to keep on our side, the partners of friends we'd like to keep. By timeboxing our conversations, we can maintain these crucial connections without being inauthentic or draining our energy reserves.

Here are some simple ways to timebox your next conversation:

- **Set a time limit up front.** In secure relationships where trust has been established, being honest about what you can commit to is an easy way to timebox the conversation. Letting our conversation partner in on our thinking frees us from the stress of wondering how we will later move things along and establishes clear expectations for our conversation partner for how to best use our time together (*I only have twenty minutes to chat, but I'm all ears until then!*).

- **Pick a spot with time constraints.** Sometimes, being candid about our intention to timebox can backfire—if the relationship is not a close one, setting a limit up front can appear ungenerous, or put undue pressure on our conversation partners to spit it out quickly. Instead, you can try a more subtle, but equally effective, approach by taking a conversation somewhere with time constraints already built in. For example, you can proactively curb time with the co-worker who talks too much by choosing the right location: instead of grabbing lunch at the office cafeteria where lingering is the norm, hit up a local restaurant where tables must turn over quickly. Avoid meeting in your office's communal spaces, which can be used for long periods of time, and aim for conference rooms that must be reserved on a limited basis instead. When you design the conversation to have a little pressure on the back end, you build in a clear conclusion to the conversation (and encourage efficiency)—without anyone's feelings getting hurt (*Looks like we are getting booted from this conference room. We'll pick this up again next week!*).

- **Schedule a conflict for afterward.** If neither of the aforementioned tactics are possible, create your own time constraints to ease your way out of the conversation. For instance, schedule an appointment, a phone call home, or even a train you cannot miss in advance to bookend your conversation. When you have a real conflict, it's easier to say so up front, and harder to feel guilty about ending the conversation (*I'm excited to catch up. I have until 2 P.M. before I need to leave for an appointment.*).

- **Set an alarm.** OK, so you probably don't need a reminder to timebox your conversation, but having an audible alarm go off can serve as an obvious cue for your conversation partner to know that it's time to go. This works particularly well at the office, where others are not likely to pry about what your alarm is really for. When it inevitably goes off in conversation, excuse yourself with a simple "I have to get going now" and move on. No one but you needs to know what this alarm has been set for.

Take a Time-Out

Like many couples, when it comes to conflict resolution, my husband and I have very different styles: when an argument gets heated

I am inclined to repair the relationship as rapidly as possible, while he prefers to first take a break and then talk through the conflict for as long as is necessary. He has great energy for this task—but it's an amount of energy I can't match. After an hour of dissecting language, tone of voice, and feelings, I am spent, and he's just getting started.

Early in our relationship, I would try to press forward and carry on. It was important to me that we repair, and if this was the way through, so be it. I recall a number of arguments resolved over hours of conversation on our living room couch, or in the car during a long road trip. These conversations were in some ways a success—we did resolve things, after all. At the same time, this way of repairing was draining for me, and I often felt exhausted by the end—too exhausted to even appreciate that we had made progress and resolved our conflict.

Over the years, I've learned that instead of forcing myself to keep going, I can be honest and clear about when I need to end the conversation. We've been together long enough that I can say, "I want to keep talking about this, but I need to hit pause. I'm not thinking clearly anymore."

Time-out requests are composed of two parts: an explicit bid to stop and the context for your appeal. They work by being clear about your need to exit the conversation and explain why, to prevent hurting your conversation partner's feelings. Time-outs are essential to easing us out of our most heated discussions, when emotions are overwhelming and the safety of either party is at stake.

Asking for a time-out works best in conversations with those with whom you already have a certain amount of intimacy and can actually strengthen your connection. By being honest with our conversation partner, we show that we trust they will understand where we are coming from; we show the same honesty and vulnerability we hope they'll share with us, too.

Consider, for instance, the following phrases:

- I hate to do this, but I think I need to stop. I am exhausted and having a hard time focusing.
- This conversation is important to me, but I'm having trouble hearing you at the moment.
- I think I need a breather—I'm noticing how charged this is for me.
- I can tell this conversation is getting the best of me. I need a time-out.

When possible, we can also give others a heads-up on when we will be ready to return to the topic.

- I want to make sure I get this right and need some time to think through it. Can we pick this back up tomorrow?
- I need a bit more time to make sure I've understood your position fully. Mind if we come back to this in an hour?
- I think I know what you mean, but I'm not 100% certain how I feel about it. Can we keep talking about this next week?

Use a Diversion

Not every relationship is strong enough to sustain candor. In these instances, less is more when it comes to quickly extricating ourselves from an otherwise draining conversation. Enter: diversions.

I had known for a while that my co-worker Les and I lived in the same neighborhood, but it wasn't until a year into working together that we actually ran into each other outside of the office. It was a Sunday afternoon at our local grocery store, me in my dog-walking shoes and need-to-do-a-load-of-laundry outfit, him sporting his newborn and looking tired but determined to do his weekend shopping. I'm not sure I would have recognized him had he not flagged me down first.

"Hey!" Les said enthusiastically. I suspect I might have been the first co-worker he'd seen in months, given he was on paternity leave. We exchanged pleasantries about his time off and the new babe, and just as I thought we might part ways, he launched in with a half dozen questions about how things were going at the office.

I wanted to be polite, but my basket of Sunday goodies was getting heavy, and I could see out of the corner of my eye a long line forming at the cash register. Also, based on my personal history with Les, I knew he had a habit of being a gossip at work, and I didn't want to contribute to any fodder. So when Les suggested we finish food shopping and grab coffee next door to catch up, I had to make a choice: give him more of my time, energy, and mental space or exit to the safety and privacy of my own home.

Because he and I aren't close, I did not feel comfortable being completely and utterly frank with him, but I wasn't about to lose my

Sunday, either. In cases like these, a *diversion*—simple, polite, and unequivocal—works best. "That sounds so nice," I said. "But unfortunately, I've really got to run." "Of course!" he said. "Nice seeing you!"

Diversions work by suggesting you can no longer talk because a competing priority or activity requires your attention. These phrases are designed to make the reason a conversation has to end more about you than the other person. They can be specific (*I need to go walk my dog.*) or vague (*I have to get going now.*), but generally, the less specific the better. Keep it courteous and to the point.

Here are a few examples:

- I have to get going now, but it was good to see you.
- I won't take up more of your time now; I'd better go.
- I'd love to talk some more, but I'm really late.
- I'm sure you're very busy, so I'll let you go now.

Interrupt

Not too long ago I was camped out at a busy coffee shop, enjoying my time the way I usually do in these settings: writing, hydrating, and observing others. A young couple sat down next to me. It was the woman's birthday, and she and her boyfriend were charting out the day's activities together (birthday breakfast, farmer's market for birthday dinner pickings, afternoon museum stroll, dinner party). The agenda was a full one, and they seemed excited about how to spend the day.

Just as the two prepared to leave, a friend came in. Gregarious and friendly, she pulled up a seat to join them. Within seconds, her presence changed the energy at the table. The girlfriend shrank ever so slightly in her seat, while the boyfriend perked up. The friend was animated and talkative, and in a few short minutes, the rest of the coffee shop and I had already learned her name, profession, romantic history, and weekend plans.

It quickly became apparent that the couple's plans would be derailed. The boyfriend and his lady friend were deep in conversation, his girlfriend chiming in from time to time but mostly bearing witness to the others' connection. She tried but failed to redirect the conversation multiple times: in no less than fifteen minutes, she had thrice suggested to her boyfriend that they get going (*What a funny story! We'd love to hear more, but we should probably get going.*). Each time she was lightly acknowledged (*Yes, we should go soon.*) or completely ignored.

It was clear that there were two different conversations happening at once—the birthday girl's bid to depart, and the friends' bid to connect—and they were directly in conflict.

Sometimes it is not enough to wait for an opening in conversation. If we are running out of time or energy and our conversation partner is still running with the mic, we may have to elbow our way in and politely interrupt. Although the birthday girl had expressed aloud her desire to get going, she had done so quietly, and in the stream of conversation, her bid went unheard. She needed to break from the others' conversation and clearly say, "I hate to interrupt, but we need to get going now." Standing up and pushing her chair in could have helped, too.

Earlier, we talked about the perils of interrupting: how it can derail a conversation, cause a missed connection, and prevent us from listening with empathy. But when we are out of time and in a rush, facing danger and need to protect ourselves, have a constraint to manage that can wait no longer, or have reached our personal limit for the conversation, interrupting becomes a necessary form of self-advocacy, a way to say "that's enough" and protect ourselves— and prevent ruined birthday plans.

To effectively interject, we must get over our discomfort, call it like it is, and admit we are interrupting. Consider the following phrases:

- I'm so sorry to interrupt, but I have a meeting I need to get to.

- I'm sorry to have to hit pause here, but I really have to get going.

- Pardon the interruption, but we really must take off now.

- Excuse me for interrupting, but I don't feel comfortable discussing this right now.

- Apologies, but I have to stop you there—I'm not ready to address this at the moment.

Acknowledge It's Over

I had been mentoring Ana for nearly six months when I hit a breaking point. Twice a month, we would meet to talk about her job and troubleshoot any problem spots. Her goal was to make a career switch, so we had discussed what was making her unhappy in her current role and what she wanted to do about it.

And yet, six months later, Ana hadn't taken action. She brought fresh complaints to me in every session, but she couldn't seem to take matters into her own hands. It wasn't for lack of opportunity: there were many equally impactful, well-paying jobs available in her field. But despite playing out potential options, Ana remained in a state of indecision. Or fear. Or guilt. Something was getting in the way, and it was clear that it wasn't going to get solved in our mentorship sessions.

There are times when we are out of our depth to help our conversation partner, as I was realizing I was with Ana. Despite my best efforts, she was stuck—and I had reached a limit. She would need to turn inward to understand what was blocking her, and I couldn't do that work for her. My empathetic ear was no longer serving either of us. So when Ana fired up the job dissatisfaction engine again during one of our sessions, I intervened.

"Ana," I said quietly. "We've been talking about your unhappiness at work for a long time. We've brainstormed possible actions, like exploring other roles internally, or looking externally. We've talked about finding joy and fulfillment outside of work and letting your job be just a job. Still, things haven't changed for you." I paused to let this sink in. Ana sighed and nodded.

"I know. I'm just still lost. I don't know what to do," she said.

"I understand," I told her, having been there myself before, "but I worry our conversations aren't helping. And if I'm honest, it's getting harder for me to talk about, too. Maybe I'm not the right person to talk to about this."

When I shared my limits with Ana, she understood—and agreed.

We were then able to talk about what—besides my mentorship—could help her move forward, and we amicably paused our mentoring relationship until Ana was ready to take action.

Sometimes, one or both parties' expectations for a conversation become misaligned. A young college grad may want help from his parents negotiating a job offer, but the generational difference and variability among industries may make their advice irrelevant. An incoming apartment resident may be interested to know more about the building's green features, and the front desk may understand little of these details. A new parent may be desperate for guidance on how to soothe a fussy newborn, while their friend may have a peaceful, easy baby and have little advice to contribute. If your conversation partner's needs can't be met given your life experience, expertise, or knowledge base, acknowledging when the conversation is falling short can move it in the right direction—even if that means moving on without you.

Though it may be painful to acknowledge when we are no longer able to continue a conversation, doing so is a generous gesture: when we can't see it ourselves, it is helpful to be shown where we are at. It may feel like we are quitting on our conversation partner when they need us most, but being honest about when we are maxed out can open new paths to meeting their needs, *outside* of just us. Redirecting in this way means placing responsibility back in our conversation partner's hands—exactly where it belongs.

The following phrases can help:

- I'm afraid I'm not being helpful here. I wonder if we should look elsewhere to make progress.

- We've done some good work here. To get to the next level, I'd recommend reaching out to someone with more [relevant history, expertise, etc.].

- It sounds like . . . is still on your mind. Perhaps it's time to [seek input elsewhere, take a break from the issue, etc.].

- It seems like your question remains unanswered. What if we [bring someone in for more guidance, take more time to reflect, try a different approach] instead?

- I can tell this dilemma is staying with you. Might it be worth . . . ?

Distance Yourself

Silvia and I have been friends since college, and though we've never been particularly close, we've stayed in touch intermittently over the years. When I first moved to San Francisco, I saw a lot of Silvia. She was one of the few people I knew in town, we were both single at the time, and she was always up for hanging out. I, too, was happy to have the company.

At first, spending time with Silvia was great. She was my ever-reliable happy hour partner in crime, my go-to pal for trying a new restaurant, and a welcome companion for exploring the city. But after a few months, I realized that my outings with Silvia often left me feeling worse off than when I started. When we talked, it was mostly about her and the things she was struggling with at the time: relationship, work, family, and roommates. I tried to be a good friend and lend a supportive ear. But the more time I spent with Silvia, the more exhausting I found it to be around her. After our conversations, I not only had less energy for myself but also much less patience and empathy for others.

It took me a while—longer than I'd like to admit—to realize that I was Silvia's crutch. Worse, if I was honest with myself, though my intentions were good, I probably wasn't helping her very much. Even a compassionate ear can be a danger, and looking back on it, my empathy may have served as enablement. (Buddhists call this "idiot compassion," when our support for others helps *us* feel better but may not be serving the other person.) My goodwill may have inadvertently enabled her to remain negative without doing much to change her circumstances.

Eventually, something had to give. I made a deliberate effort to reduce our interactions. Over time, I politely declined Silvia's invitations to spend time together and reached out to her less and less. We now see each other just a few times a year, enough for us to enjoy each other's company but not so much that we fall into negativity.

In extreme cases, ending a conversation isn't enough—you might also need to end the relationship. If you notice that you are dreading speaking with an individual, leaving conversations feeling lethargic and disinterested in hobbies that normally excite you, or questioning your self-worth because of your interactions with someone, it may be time to reassess the relationship. *Distancing*, the act of progressively reducing interactions with our conversation partner, may be the way out.

This technique is especially helpful when we are in the presence of those I call *takers*—the people in our lives who, intentionally or not, take energy from us in conversation but never give it back. This behavior typically looks like monologuing (talking about oneself at length), venting (giving voice to one's feelings, often as a complaint or in frustration), or confessing (sharing deeply personal and sometimes difficult stories).

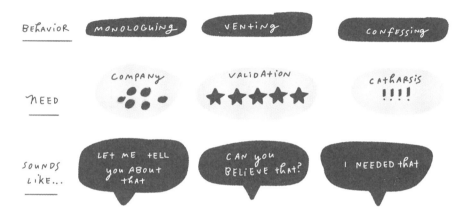

None of these behaviors are inherently bad. It's natural to seek the company of others when we want to stop feeling lonely, feel newly reassured, or unburden ourselves of trauma. And truth be told, even those of us who swear we'd *never* be a taker have probably been a taker at one time or another. But in their quest to feel better, this group can be *so* zoned in on having their needs met that they do not hear or see their conversation partner. They are so inward-focused that they fail to intuit that we, *too*, might need to express ourselves in conversation.

Some people "take" only from time to time—when they are stressed or otherwise preoccupied and not on their best or most empathetic behavior. Others, like Silvia was with me, are repeat offenders—they consistently take more than they give in conversation and, worse, learn to keep coming back to the same empathetic ears when they realize how good they feel coming out of those conversations. (If I always feel recharged after talking to you, I am going to want more of that.) Along with the other exit strategies discussed earlier, when possible, distancing is particularly useful for managing this group.

When called for, you can create distance by following these steps:

- **Reduce interactions.** Declining social outings or work lunches may seem extreme, but is it, if your well-being is at stake? Assuming it's an option, reduce how frequently you see your conversation partner. Schedule meetings with a certain co-worker once a month instead of once a week, and push your monthly happy hour with a certain friend to quarterly.

- **Generate space.** Notice how quickly you respond to your conversation partner. Do you answer their every beck and call right away? Try to pause before you instinctively respond to that text or email. If it's not urgent, give yourself space to breathe first.

- **Be open to changing course.** Guess what? Your conversation partner may notice that you are creating distance. (If they do not, you might take that as evidence that you've made the right choice.) If they do and follow up with you (*I've noticed you haven't been available lately. Is everything OK?*), consider this an olive branch. Pick up the call, accept the dinner invite, meet for that coffee, and see if continuing to distance yourself from this relationship still makes sense.

BRING ON THE ENERGIZERS

As you prune your conversations—and your relationships—be sure to balance out your days and moments with those whose company you *do* wish to keep. Specifically, keep the line open to *energizers*. In contrast to takers, who demand more from us than they are able or willing to return, energizers are those in our lives who uplift, inspire, and listen to us with empathy as much as (and sometimes more than) we listen to them. They are our sounding boards for when we work through a personal problem and the perfect collaborators when we need to brainstorm at work. They give us their full attention, listen and ask questions, follow up, proactively check in, and give us the space to express *our* needs. Their authentic curiosity in us leaves us feeling refreshed and recharged in conversation.

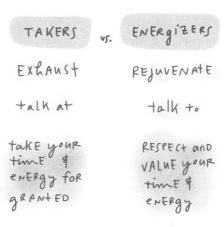

TAKERS   vs.   ENERGIZERS

EXHAUST   REJUVENATE

talk at   talk to

takE your   RESPECT and
time &   VALUE your
energy for   time &
gRANtED   energy

If we're lucky, we have more energizers than takers in our lives. But sometimes—because we feel too guilty or loyal to distance ourselves from unhealthy relationships, or don't know how to—without realizing it, circumstances are such that the energizers are outnumbered. That's why it's extra important to find balance and ensure that we, too, are supported: Take the time to cultivate these important relationships and prioritize reconnecting with this group if ties have begun to weaken. Be there for them just as they are for you. Let them know—through your actions and your words—that you value their company and the empathetic listening they bring to your conversations.

EXERCISE: Conduct a Relationship Audit

In an ideal world, our relationships are well balanced and our time and energy is evenly distributed among our friends, co-workers, and family. But I don't know anyone who doesn't have at least one relationship in their life that needs some work. This becomes an even greater risk as we become better listeners.

Luckily, we can tip the scales back in our favor. To do this, answer the following questions to see who in your life is a taker and who is an energizer. As you do, think about the history of conversations you have had with an individual overall. By looking at things in the aggregate, we can find patterns of behavior.

- Name the friends, co-workers, and family members in your life who generally leave you more exhausted than refreshed, with whom conversations often make you tired. Then, list those who replenish your cup and leave you feeling motivated and energized. Why might that be?

- Thinking of the people in your life most available to you—because they are physically nearby (such as neighbors, roommates, or office mates) or frequently able to chat even at a distance (like the friend who always picks up your call no matter the time of day)—how many of these relationships are serving their purpose? Of the people in your life you *communicate* with the most, with whom do you actually *connect*?

- Taking stock of your list, do you have the right combination of energizing versus draining relationships in your life? Be honest with yourself about how things are shaking out.

- Reflecting on your relationships with takers, what are some of the reasons you tend to give so much (guilt, duty, a feeling of helplessness to turn things around, etc.)? Knowing your own tendencies here will serve you in managing these relationships in the future.

- Looking at those who energize you, what characterizes those relationships and conversations? How do these energizers make you feel heard? Knowing when you feel heard is just as powerful as knowing when you don't.

BEFORE YOU FORGET

Sometimes we have to call it. When a conversation can no longer be redirected, has become unsafe, or has drained our energy reserves, empathetic listening becomes impossible, and our best bet may be to end the conversation. As your listening skills improve, you may have to do this more often: more people may seek you out for your kind ear, and more frequently, and you will need to draw the line.

CHAPTER 10

Difficult Conversations

B y now, dear reader, you have tackled much of what is required to cultivate your listening practice. You've learned how to start a conversation on the right foot, and how to navigate it as it unfolds. You know how to stay attentive to others in conversation, and how to decode nonverbal cues in the moment. You've explored how to bring your best questions to the conversation, make space for others, and ensure you understand what you're hearing. You've learned how to gently guide others where they need to go and even end a conversation when it's called for. Still, despite our best efforts, certain circumstances can make empathetic listening all the more difficult.

The most common hurdles to listening are environmental, relational, and topical. In this chapter, we'll go over how to mitigate distractions, manage unwieldy relationships, and navigate even the most sensitive subjects in conversation.

Environmental Hurdles

We have all been there. Perhaps you are the type of person who simply cannot help but look at a TV screen if it's in your line of sight, even if you don't mean to. Maybe you are juggling your child's needs and your own simultaneously. Or maybe you've been unable to keep up with your conversation partner while in a loud restaurant or have been interrupted by your phone or other device.

Unfortunately for us, distractions are a dime a dozen and can hinder our ability to listen with empathy: the more distractions, the less patient, engaged, and understanding we tend to be. But the good news is that they can be managed—once we become aware of them. With attention, dedicated practice, and a willingness to share our intent with those around us, we can take control of environmental hurdles.

Here are some common distractions in conversation and how to navigate them.

LITTLE ONES (CHILDREN, PETS)

Anyone with a child or pet in their life knows they can provide much-loved moments of play, fun, and wonder. But no matter how much you love their company, it can be hard to have a deep one-on-one in the presence of an adventurous young one or spirited pet. Besides being distracting, it can be very easy to slip into a conversation that becomes exclusively about these little ones if we aren't careful (*He's growing up so fast! . . . I know, just the other day, he did this amazing thing all by himself . . .*). If you or your conversation partner are struggling to balance the little ones you love with the adult connection you need, there are a few things you can do:

- **Arrange to fly solo.** When possible, call in for backup (a sitter, grandparents, dog boarding, etc.) so you can go it alone on occasion. Make sure your conversation partner does the same so that neither of you feel guilty or distracted during your conversation. When making personal sacrifices like these, it helps to be on equal footing.

- **Keep the littles busy.** Sometimes leaving pets and children at home or with a caregiver isn't an option, but this doesn't mean every activity needs to be centered on them. Choose an activity that can facilitate your intention to connect in conversation, such as visiting dog parks, playgrounds, and other locales that allow for free play without active involvement from adults.

- **Invite them in.** Having a conversation in the midst of little ones can at times feel like an inconvenience, but it can also be a sign of a strong relationship. What can we learn from how our conversation partner relates to their loved ones? Children, pets, and others we take care of can bring to light a side of our conversation partner we may not often see, like their playful spirit, their vulnerabilities, or even their raw frustration. These are often private, even tender moments, so recognize that you are being let in on something special and embrace it.

PICK A PLACE aND Activity wHERE EVERYONE hAS A joB

GRASS iNSPEC+OR

INSEC+ EXPLORER

EMPA+hE+ic LiS+ENERS

BACKGROUND NOISE

Concerts, bars, and loud restaurants all have their place in our so-cial lives at one age or another, but we should be judicious about the kinds of conversations we attempt to have there. When we are in a loud environment, our listening efforts are diverted to deciphering *what* is being said, rather than why, making it difficult to connect beyond the surface. Besides having to work hard to hear others, these circumstances can prove emotionally trying: repeatedly strain-ing to hear can be frustrating. A few minutes of "What did you say?" can be all it takes to discourage us from having the kinds of inti-mate conversations we seek. By the time our conversation partner comes in loud and clear, we may have little patience or energy to be the empathetic listener they deserve.

On the other hand, complete quiet can also prove challenging, especially if you are in a public setting, like a co-working space, coffee shop, or museum. It may be challenging to be vulnerable in this setting: what if you don't particularly *want* everyone in the room to hear your personal news, or that of your conversation partner? At the risk of others overhearing, you may be inclined to rush through your conversation and miss out on deepening a connection. Instead, you can:

- **Be selective about your meeting spots.** Aim for a location that can foster the conversations you seek. Take a Goldilocks approach—not too loud, not too quiet—and pick an environment that neither stokes frustration nor inhibits vulnerability. The goal is to be confident that you can receive and respond to others with ease as you listen.

- **Consider privacy.** Not every conversation requires complete privacy, but some do. Think twice before taking on a tricky relationship conversation at a restaurant or a performance review in an open office space. Instead, try parks or other locales that offer both privacy and ambient noise at once.

- **Don't be afraid to pivot.** Should you wind up at a restaurant that looks great but has deafening acoustics or in an office corner that is far too quiet for a difficult conversation, no need to suffer through it; find a new place and tell your conversation partner why you're suggesting it. (The better to hear you, my dear.) Adapting in this way demonstrates care and allows us to be available to others.

DEVICES

In her book *Reclaiming Conversation*, Sherry Turkle, a psychologist specializing in the relationship between people and technology, notes that even the mere presence of a device in our view during conversation can lead to disconnection. As a result, our conversations stay on the surface, our willingness to be vulnerable decreases, our capacity for empathy is inhibited, and we feel less connected to each other.[1]

Whether you put yourself squarely in the Luddite camp, nostalgic for the phone-free days that were, or happily on the side of technologists aiming to change the world for the better, we can all admit that we're a tad more distracted by devices than we used to be. To foster greater empathy, we need to reduce the presence of screens when possible. Below are a few ways to do that.

- **Set devices aside.** Silence your phone, close laptops, and put screens aside. Keep them out of sight to minimize distractions.

- **Encourage others to do the same.** Instead of expressing this as a demand, explain why you are taking this approach; this shows your conversation partner that you are putting them first and nudges them to do the same. You can even create a designated zone for devices, like a phone jar or box to keep the group's phones from interrupting conversation.

- **Build willpower.** Resist the urge to google during conversation or "just shoot off a quick email" as you talk. (Do you really need to know the year that movie came out right now? Can that message really not wait?) Remember, every break in conversation you introduce becomes a gap you must bridge to connection.

Relational Hurdles

Controlling for our environment is one thing; controlling for our relationships is an entirely different beast. Some hurdles are born more from how we relate to our conversation partner than where we physically speak with them. Certain relationships place us and our conversation partners in particular roles that affect our way of seeing and listening to each other. These roles can be determined by power dynamics, how intimately we know our conversation partner, how competitive we are with each other, or even cultural differences. Once these roles are in place, it can be hard to break out of them. Rest assured, these hurdles, common as they are, are surmountable.

HIERARCHICAL RELATIONSHIPS

Early in my career, I heard about a manager who believed certain challenges were appropriate for certain stages of one's career—meaning that if you were a senior employee, you should not be asking "junior-level" questions. Of course, it seemed fair to expect that people should grow as they gained more experience, but this standard also seemed subjective: Who besides him could know what "junior-level" meant?

When a senior researcher I admired shared a story about a question he'd asked that this manager had swatted down, I was surprised. This was a tenured researcher and respected mentor to his team. He had built strong relationships, and his work was high-caliber. And *he* was being told his questions weren't sophisticated enough? (I could only imagine if it had been me: What if I, a junior researcher aspiring toward midcareer, asked something that not even a junior researcher should ask? What if it turned out my questions were [*gasp!*] *intern* level?)

The result of this policy was that the researcher saved most of his questions for his peers, who he knew wouldn't judge him. It was too risky for him to ask his manager, the keeper of the keys on promotions, bonuses, and other opportunities, when he needed help— one "junior" question could put all of that out of reach.

This strategy saved him from embarrassment, but it also meant that his manager never really got to know him. When the researcher finally left for another company, I wasn't surprised to hear he felt no qualms about his decision; he hadn't felt safe enough to ask questions that he knew would help him grow, so leaving felt like the obvious choice. I knew then that the relationship had truly failed— perhaps if they had developed a more honest relationship, the departure would have been harder to swallow.

A key characteristic of hierarchical relationships like this one is an imbalance of power. In these relationships, one person is an authority figure and the other is not. When the playing field is uneven, it can be hard to be honest, and each side can wind up on the offensive. Because honesty can be used against those with little power, they may hold back or project intentions onto what the authority in the relationship says. (This is why we so often hear about leaders having to "earn the trust" of those they work with.) Even those with ample power may have cause to withhold and fear being honest, as doing so can degrade their clout and authority. (This is why some leaders, celebrities, and even parents may avoid admitting their mistakes or making authentic apologies.)

To navigate hierarchical relationships, we can:

- **Even out the playing field.** If you are in the "more powerful" role, strive to create a safe space for others to share without fear of judgment or misunderstanding. We can do so by modeling this behavior ourselves: when we show a willingness to be honest, our conversation partner is more likely to respond in kind. We can also invite others to be honest with us and thank them when they have been vulnerable in sharing their feedback.

  If you are in the "less dominant" role, think of your conversation partner not as a vice president, boss, teacher, manager, etc., but more like a fellow human. This doesn't mean respecting them any less, but it does mean shifting how we relate to them. When we redefine our relationship to be less about status and more about others as individuals, we are likely to be less intimidated and more open as a result.

- **Ask yourself what you are afraid of.** When we don't trust others, we hear everything they say through the lens of our distrust. Ask yourself: What's driving my distrust? What might I be nervous about or uncomfortable with? For instance, does every politically savvy and ambitious co-worker rub you the wrong way, or just this one? Do you distrust this doctor in particular, or all doctors? Articulating our fears becomes useful information, since now we can do something about it.

REGRESSIVE RELATIONSHIPS

Ever notice how you're never on your best behavior at home? Like it or not, our families often see both the best and the worst of us. They are privy to the sides of us we keep tucked away from friends and co-workers, the parts of our personality we may be less than proud of. And no matter how old we get, the bad habits and old attitudes we thought we grew out of can come back to us like second nature when we are around family.

This return to the mean is due to what psychologists call "family systems theory," the idea that each family member fulfills a role in keeping the family in equilibrium.[2] "Equilibrium" looks different for every family, but it is what drives one sibling to play the role of jokester while another embraces the role of the pacifier, and still another acts as the perpetually sullen teenager. We may have worked hard to shed these roles outside of our families, but returning to our family "system" often puts us right back into these roles in order to keep the family "in balance."

RED ROVER, RED ROVER, SEND yoNR iNNER fivE-yEAR-OLd OVER

Not only do *we* regress into our younger selves, but we also expect those around us to do the same. We may hear things through the filter of a memory (*She's always given me a hard time about that.*) or a learned expectation (*He's going to give me grief about this, I know it.*). Suddenly, a need can sound like a demand, a joke like a criticism, a request like a judgment, or an observation like an attack. Our tainted perception of others makes it hard to listen to them clearly.

Regressive dynamics aren't just limited to family, either; many of our relationships have a similar "equilibrium" in place. Think about your team at work or group of close friends. You can probably recognize any number of "types" within the group: the do-gooder, the slacker, the creative, the genius, and more. As with family, roles are relative to the group: once a slot has been filled, there is no room for another. We may even unconsciously search for groups that reinforce our previously adopted roles and family patterns.

Empathetic listening in regressive relationships must clear multiple hurdles: When we expect our conversation partner to fill a particular role in the group or to show up in a certain way, we make it harder for ourselves to really hear them. When we are pushed to perform a particular role within the group, we do not fare much better. If we behave in ways we haven't since childhood and expect others to do the same, we often scratch against painful and deep-seated fears that make listening with empathy much harder.

The next time a family member, teammate, or friend inadvertently brings out the worst of you in conversation, try these strategies:

- **Pick your battles.** Be judicious about when you want to go down the emotional rabbit hole. Sometimes it's better to apologize and acknowledge your role in escalating the conversation so that you can quickly recalibrate and get back to listening.

- **Hit pause.** Take a break, take a walk. Pushing our buttons is a talent our closest relations are best at. Acknowledge what's happening and give yourself a healthy breather—especially when you're the one pushing the buttons.

- **Remind yourself of their good qualities.** In the heat of the moment, try to draw on a fond memory of your adversary to calm yourself down. It sometimes helps to call upon a memory of others *as a child*—children are usually a lot harder to get mad at than adults.

- **Check your filters.** Try to objectively understand if your reaction is a function of the day's stressors, emotions, family roles, or other relationship dynamics. What's causing your outsize reaction? What filter might you be listening through? Acknowledging how you are feeling and identifying where it's coming from can help you return to neutral.

COMPETITIVE RELATIONSHIPS

There's one in every office: the colleague who regularly gets the limelight for the same tasks you dutifully fulfill but have never been thanked for (*What gives?*). Or maybe you've found yourself bragging about your child when you run into that one neighbor (*My daughter is studying medicine. At Yale.*). Had an irrationally judgmental thought about someone's style, point of view, or achievements (*She thinks she looks so great today, doesn't she? Lame.*)? Whether we are aware of it or not, these may be signs that we are in a competitive relationship.

Competitive relationships occur when we measure our achievements against someone else's and aspire to meet and surpass them. Sometimes, it's obvious to us that we are doing this: we want to be promoted over our co-worker, get the better grades, or win the important client. Other times it's less obvious: we want to be well liked, like a popular friend we have. We want to be rewarded and validated at work so that others can see how good we are at our job. We want to stand out for our personal style and find ourselves in a constant unwitting game of "Who Wore It Better?" We want to do as our role models have done in work, love, parenting, and beyond.

Competitive relationships are not born of rationality but of insecurity. For example, even how women give birth, an experience that comes down more to luck and genetics than skill or effort, can have some mothers trying to best each other. Some compete on victory (*No epidural here! Only six hours of labor! No tearing!*). Some compete on pain (*Twenty hours? That's terrible, and I should know, mine lasted thirty-two hours. Thirty-two hours? That's tough. Mine was sixty.*). It's hard to say who wins in any of these scenarios, and yet, the conversations remain strangely competitive.

Even though we can't control our body's pain threshold or dilation rate, how "good" of a sleeper our child is, how fast our metabolism or how athletic our body is, we can still harbor feelings of jealousy, inadequacy, and insecurity about them. And when someone does these things "better" than us—well, we can't help but take notice and compare ourselves.

In order to listen with empathy in competitive relationships, we will have to:

- **Interrogate our feelings.** Do you really dislike and disdain the other person, or could this be a masked insecurity? Is it really that you hate the way this person holds themselves in conversation, or is this a talent that you subconsciously admire and wish you had yourself? Unraveling what's behind our competitive feelings can help us see them for what they are (feelings!) and better manage them as a result.

- **Quiet our judgment.** Passing judgment is easy to do when you are feeling competitive, but ultimately unproductive. When you hear Lady Judgment rearing her self-righteous head, ask her to quiet down. Acknowledge what you are feeling, name these feelings for what they are, and move on (*OK, self-righteousness, that's enough.*).

- **Remind ourselves of our shared humanity.** In competitive relationships, it can be very easy to demonize the other person and, consequently, completely ignore or disregard what they have to say. It is much harder to recognize that, like us, our competitors are humans with flaws and insecurities and emotional foibles. This type of insight can make it much easier to listen with empathy.

CROSS-CULTURAL RELATIONSHIPS

Have a conversation with most native New Yorkers and you'll quickly learn they have no problem interjecting. In fact, this kind of conversation style is often a sign of engagement, a way of showing they are interested in what you have to say and are excited to partake. In other parts of the country, this behavior might be considered, well, rude. Depending on your upbringing, you may be more likely to wait until a pause in conversation before interjecting—no problem, right? Except that a New Yorker may misinterpret silence as a sign of disinterest. (As a New Yorker married to a Midwesterner, I can personally attest to this kind of confusion.)

Deborah Tannen is a linguist who has studied everyday conversation extensively. Her research suggests that how we engage in the "rhythm" of conversation itself can be culturally driven, as when there are regional differences, like with my husband and me, and that habits as simple as how we signal that we are listening can even vary across genders.[3] For example, women tend to say "mm-hmm" to express acknowledgment in conversation, but men are more likely to interpret this as agreement. These subtle differences can have outsize effects: a friend may feel slighted by what he perceived as support but you meant as confirmation you were listening, a pregnant pause can leave you wondering if your boss will go up to bat for you in this next promotion cycle, and even a simple misunderstanding can quickly escalate into an argument.

Having friends, family, and co-workers who are different from us is part of what makes life and meeting people so interesting. But as enriching as it can be to surround ourselves with those of diverse backgrounds and life experiences, it's also true that we may have to work extra hard to listen with empathy when our conversation styles and reference points are so varied.

To keep your listening chops strong no matter the company, here are a few tactics to keep in mind:

- **Be aware of cultural differences.** Not every New Yorker is an interrupter, nor do all men interpret "mm-hmm" as agreement. But differences in upbringing *can* influence the roles we play in conversation. Remind yourself not to assume that you are speaking the same language (even if, quite literally, you are).

- **Explore what makes others unique.** When you encounter a dissimilarity in style, instead of dismissing it as negative, acknowledge it and explore it. What can you learn about your conversation partner based on their signaling habits and speech cadence? What might their conversation style tell you about them? Approaching conversations with curiosity enables us to listen with empathy.

- **Ask for clarity.** As you notice differences in conversation style, you may develop theories about what they mean (*Oh, when she says "mm-hmm," she's being polite, not agreeing.*). Remember that you can always confirm your hypotheses by asking your conversation partner directly.

Topical Hurdles

We can all agree that certain conversation topics are almost universally benign, like talking about the weather. But there are also what I call *high-friction* topics: topics that get us riled up and hit against our deepest emotions, passions, values, and beliefs, such as politics, religion, child-rearing philosophies, or even sports. Whether personal, cultural, or societal, these topics tend to evoke strong feelings that can make listening with empathy more difficult.

We could try to avoid these topics altogether, but that isn't always possible—once ignored or averted, they are increasingly at the forefront of many of our everyday conversations. Nor is that approach recommended—in my experience, avoidance has a way of heightening the stakes. At the risk of censoring ourselves or others, we can, with a little attention, navigate these topics successfully.

TABOO TOPICS

Rita had been through a lot. Before the pandemic hit, she had been a successful freelance videographer, known for her work at conferences, weddings, festivals, and events large and small. But when Minnesota's stay-at-home order went into effect, her income stream quickly dried up. People weren't hiring videographers for weddings anymore, and events were on hold indefinitely. For our research session, I needed to learn how Rita was adjusting to her new reality, but I would have to do so carefully and supportively.

To navigate this fraught and deeply personal subject, I let Rita know that today's session might be difficult, and that we could stop at any time. My goal, I said, was to get to know her experience—with all its peaks and valleys—which meant that I might ask some questions that made her uncomfortable. It was important that she understood these questions came from a good place and were not meant to provoke her in any way. "OK," Rita said, nodding. "I'll do my best."

I turned to a favorite research tool of mine that I hoped would make it easier for Rita to safely tell her story: an *emotion map*. An emotion map is a tool to help participants express their emotions as they relate to a sequence of events. On a piece of paper, participants plot out the various steps of a process, workflow, or journey (*After you filed for unemployment, then what happened?*), along with their emotions (*How did it feel to file for unemployment?*). Emotion maps are ideal for conversations about a complex and, as their moniker suggests, emotional series of events. There is something about drawing out our experience that makes it easier for us to talk about it.

Rita drew out her journey, from thriving freelancer to the first canceled video shoots, to filing for unemployment and taking on childcare duties full time. She plotted these turning points on the X axis, against a range of emotions on the Y axis. As she did, I gently encouraged her to think aloud, and the stories began to pour out.

"My whole identity is wrapped up in my job," she said. "And I can't do that anymore. A part of me is saying, 'You're done. It's over.'"

As I listened, I tamped down my instinct to tell her everything would be OK, because I didn't—couldn't—know that. I quieted the part of my brain that had begun concocting possible solutions and reminded myself to slow down, giving Rita the space to share what she was comfortable with and taking the necessary time to get there, without pouncing for more information or suggesting potential solutions. By the time I turned to more pointed questions on how she was managing her now dwindling finances, our rapport had been solidified.

Some subjects, like unemployment, are more difficult to talk about than others because they go up against our societal and cultural norms. *Taboo topics* are those we tend to shy away from because we've been taught—explicitly or implicitly—not to discuss them. What is considered to be taboo can evolve over time (remember when it was considered gauche to be online dating, or to show up to a job interview with visible tattoos?), but such shifts are determined by the collective—our family units, schools and offices, even pop culture—rather than the individual. This is why it can still be uncomfortable to talk about your salary with your co-workers, discuss your religious or political views with your boss, or share your experience with racism, sexism, and bias with others, even if you consider yourself to be an "open book." But these topics are only taboo because we don't talk about them regularly: not because they're bad. We'll learn how to navigate them next.

Start with a Warm-up

If I wake up tomorrow and decide to run a marathon without having ever run a mile, I'll get hurt. In the same way, because we talk about taboo topics so rarely, it can be jarring to jump right into them in conversation. We first have to warm up our voices.

In user research sessions, we bake a "warm-up" section into every interview for this very reason. We start with a few minutes of small talk and softball questions to loosen the participant (and ourselves) up. This gives participants a chance to get used to being in a lab and to get over the idea that there might be a group of people observing them behind what looks like a simple mirror.

In real life, we have the advantage of not having a voice recorder, camera, one-way mirror, or reporter's notepad to get in the way and make it harder to connect. But when emotions come into play, connecting can be just as difficult.

You can help your conversation partner warm up to discussing a taboo topic with a few simple steps:

- **Tell them in advance what you'd like to talk about.** This gives everyone a chance to mentally prepare in advance and ensures no one feels blindsided by a taboo topic. You'd appreciate the same courtesy, too.

- **Clarify your intent.** The best way to prevent the conversation from being automatically shut down is to clarify your rationale for bringing up these unwieldy issues. If a topic feels off-limits, you can make it safe for others to participate by explaining why you are broaching the subject, and by reassuring them that your goal is not to offend or push too hard. Simply stating what your intent is up front can reduce some of the fear around taboo topics. In my conversation with Rita, I let her know that things might get uncomfortable, but that my intent was not to provoke her.

- **Start small and build from there.** When it's time to talk, start from neutral ground to put everyone at ease. There's typically at least one thing you can safely agree on before your views diverge. (A manager sharing critical feedback with a direct report can admit, "I had trouble with this when I was in your role, too.") This can build confidence to tackle the harder stuff.

Summon Your Bravery

Uri Berliner is a senior business editor at NPR. Normally at work behind the scenes, he took an unusual turn in 2018 when he reported on a deeply personal story about his father. As a child, his father had been separated from his parents in Germany during the Holocaust. They eventually died in a concentration camp. Uri knew bits and pieces of his family's story, but there were many parts his father had never talked with him about. For his piece, Uri knew he would have to dig not only into his father's past but also into his own relationship with him.

Just *thinking* about broaching such a sensitive topic with a parent would be enough to stop many of us in our tracks. What if we push too far? What if we open the floodgates and can't close them again? What if our parent becomes defensive or unwilling to talk to us? These were risks Uri was going to have to take.

In his radio segment, Uri shows the upside of taking on such a difficult conversation. When he asks his father questions about his past for the first time, he is surprised to learn that, actually, his father is eager to share more.

"He was thankful to me for asking these questions, even though they were painful,"[4] Uri says. So ready was his father that, in the end, this difficult conversation strengthened their relationship and brought the pair closer together. "In a way, it's a relief. It's good. It should come out. It's a kind of a wonderful story," Uri's father said.[5]

Talking about taboo topics requires a certain degree of courage and willingness to put our fears aside. Like learning any new skill, getting started is the hardest part. Though we may expect others to shy away from difficult topics, sometimes they are more ready for them than we know. Instead of thinking of these conversations as a burden, consider that they might be the opportunity that your conversation partner has been waiting for. So summon your bravery and go for it.

To do this, you can:

- **Make a plan.** Think through how you will approach your conversation in advance. Outline the topics you want to cover and how you will broach the subject. Researchers use tools like emotion maps, but even imagining how the conversation may go can help you get the most out of it. Plot out possible reactions to prepare yourself for any outcome, including how you will know if it's time to call it quits. Think about how you will respond if things go south, or, on the flip side, even better than you expected.

- **Expect discomfort—and sit in it.** You will likely feel uncomfortable at one point or another—this is totally normal! Notice when you are uncomfortable and do your best to embrace this feeling instead of run away from it. You may feel a strong urge to ease the discomfort, as I did with Rita. Know that the more you broach these subjects over time, the less taboo they will seem to you.

- **Just do it.** Once you have warmed up your conversation partner and eased into the conversation, it's time. At a certain point, the only thing left to do is to dive right in.

Aim for Understanding, Not Agreement

Last primary season, a friend of mine quit her job to volunteer for a candidate she was passionate about. She threw herself into the work of raising money, making phone calls, sending emails, and, of course, posting on social media to get the word out about why she felt so strongly about her candidate of choice. "I don't normally get political," she would start by saying, "but this really means a lot to me."

Some people in her life were enthusiastic: they, too, supported the same candidate, or if they did not, they were at least on the same side of the political spectrum. But others were not so quick to get on board—or at all.

With one friend in particular, conversations became a battleground. "I can't believe you buy into that perspective," he would say. "Well, do you *really* think that . . . ?" my friend would counter.

This pattern continued for the better part of a summer, until my friend began to approach these conversations differently. Instead of coming out swinging and forcefully defending her candidate, she started to slow down and hear her friend out. "I appreciate your point of view. I want to know more about the other side," she said, inviting him to share more. As he felt safer to share his perspective, without fear of being lambasted for it, their conversations became decidedly more civil. Did they become best friends? No, they did not. Do they see eye to eye on politics and policy? No, they do not. But they are no longer enemies. Instead, they understand that they share more in common than they thought (*I can appreciate your feistiness and willingness to speak up. I feel that way, too.*). They still may not agree on the best candidate for the job, but they can at least understand the other person's point of view (*Even though I don't agree that . . . , I'm probably wrong when I think . . .*). This seemingly small change shifted the nature of their conversations so much that a year later, on Super Tuesday, her once adversary even reached out to wish her good luck! What made my friend's approach so effective was that she had begun to listen rather than defend.

It can be hard to comfortably hold beliefs in opposition to others, but we are being asked to do this more and more. You can see the divide within family units, classrooms, and workplaces, as well as on a global scale. These kinds of divides can wreak havoc on our ability to work together, make progress, have a nice family dinner—and listen with empathy.

The next time you're faced with a difficult conversation where values are on the line, try the following:

- **Affirm, affirm, affirm.** Show your conversation partner that you are listening and are interested in what they have to say, even if you don't agree with it. Encourage them to say more in a way that feels authentic to you, whether nonverbally (maintaining eye contact, nodding), verbally (*OK, go on*), or both. If you are known to heavily sigh, roll your eyes, or shut down at opinions that don't align with yours, do your best to curb those habits. You can support your conversation partner and affirm their existence, even if your perspectives differ.

- **Explain without convincing.** When it comes time for you to share your perspective, do so humbly and without an agenda— the goal is not to convince others that you are right. Try not to get too bogged down in specifics that can be hard for others to connect to, but share instead what informs your perspective. For example, do you support sustainable efforts because you grew up in the countryside and have fond memories of being in nature with your parents? Talk about that instead of diving into the minutiae of the Paris Climate Agreement.

- **Remember, it's not about you.** Part of what can make taboo topics like politics and religion so divisive is that they hit against our belief systems. To encounter an opposing point of view can sometimes feel like a rejection of our entire being. Remind yourself—before, during, and after the conversation—that opposing beliefs are not a rejection of you as a person. Your conversation partner has a *lifetime* of experiences they call upon to inform their beliefs—for better or for worse, your difference of opinion is but a drop in the bucket of their overall worldview. If someone does not agree with your perspective, put their reaction in context and let go of the feeling that their response means something about *you*.

Respect Your Boundaries

Should things get heated, take a deep breath and count to five. Give yourself a moment to let your nervous system calm down before continuing. If the conversation is still too charged after taking a beat, take that as useful information that this topic is a tender one for you, and it's time to stop. It is better to hit pause and return to the conversation when you are in a more neutral state than to power through and reach the point of explosion.

You are also the best judge for when a conversation has crossed a line and you *don't* want to return to it. Respect that instinct, too, and take on only what you can handle. When the conversation takes a turn for the worse, remember the exit strategies we learned in chapter 9.

HOT SPOTS

I was sitting in my local coffee shop to work on this very book when a young couple sat down at the table next to me and began to discuss their wedding plans. I tried to ignore them, but something the bride-to-be said caught my ear.

"I feel like I'm not being heard," she told her fiancé. "We keep looking at venues, but it feels like my voice isn't part of the decision-making process anymore. I've mentioned before that I'd like to get married at my parents' place, so it's disheartening to keep looking." Then, her tone took a turn, and instead of giving her partner an opening to respond, she gave him a warning: "Be careful what you say next, because you can make this a lot worse."

Oops! Though she had started out neutral, the tenor of the conversation changed immediately. There was a zing of danger in the air as the two began to tense up: Where before her fiancé appeared ready to support and troubleshoot with her, now his body language, facial expression, and tone signaled he was on the defensive. His response? A cool "I don't like these rules," and the conversation quickly devolved from there.

Hot spots are sensitive topics that scratch against memories, beliefs, and experiences we find emotionally distressing. Unlike taboo topics, they aren't necessarily about something deemed socially or culturally "inappropriate," such as talking about sexuality or salary. Instead, they are unique to every one of us and are dependent on our personal histories, individual experiences, and insecurities. Mother's Day may be a hot spot for someone with a complicated relationship with a parent, while the first day of school may be a hot spot for someone who grew up moving around a lot. That's why hot spots often appear to be much more inconsequential, at least to the untrained eye (*It's just a wedding venue, right?*), even when they're not.

Of course, there can be some overlap between taboo topics, which are established as "off-limits" at the societal level, and hot spots, which are personal danger zones for each individual; our own identities and experiences can make these already complicated topics that much more fraught. (Talking about sexism, for instance, may be awkward for everyone involved, but particularly so for someone who has personally experienced it.) This raises the stakes for listening with empathy even more.

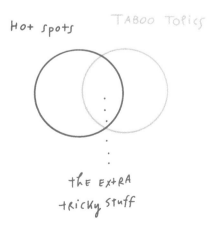

When we encounter hot spots, we quickly become emotionally charged and reactive, and it can be hard to bounce back. In these scenarios, a difference of opinion can sound like a personal rejection, an opposing point of view can feel like an affront to our core values, and even a compliment can sound hurtful when we are in a high-alert state. (*You're so intense about this right now . . . No, no, I meant that in a good way!*) These reactions can then overpower our efforts to listen with empathy.

Naturally, from the outside, it is always easier to see what is happening. Here, the soon-to-be bride wants to feel heard but pushes her fiancé away in the process. He wants to repair the situation but can't from a place of defensiveness. They try to get through to each other but are too emotionally charged to hear what the other is actually saying.

Eventually, the hot spot reveals itself. The problem, for this couple, was not just that their search for venues was discouraging. It was that the bride-to-be would find it particularly meaningful to host the wedding at her childhood home, as a symbol of her past and her future, and given the many fond memories she held there. Though her partner had meant to be helpful in exploring alternatives, his venue brainstorming sounded like rejection to her ears— a rejection of her idea and, by extension, of her and her family.

Hot spots are so unique to each individual that it can be difficult to anticipate (and prevent) them from surfacing in others. But we can work to manage our own hot spots and how they show up in conversation. Here are a few suggestions for doing so:

- **Be aware of your personal hot spots.** Knowing the topics that you are sensitive to, whether a specific memory or underlying insecurity, allows you to mentally and emotionally prepare yourself—not for battle, but for adapting your emotions as they arise. When we are on to ourselves, we can better manage our responses.

- **Meditate on it.** Ground yourself instead of letting your emotions get the best of you. Visualize a calming picture or repeat a mantra. Try, for instance: "My mind is a piece of wood," or any other phrase that helps you relax in particularly charged moments, and repeat as necessary. Take deep breaths to come back to center during an upsetting conversation.

- **Have an exit strategy.** When all else fails, it's perfectly acceptable to bail before things get worse. Recall what we learned in chapter 9 on ending the conversation, and when you've reached your threshold, call for a time-out. Plan to return to the topic when you're in a more neutral—and therefore more empathetic—state. This can also be helpful if others' hot spots have surfaced and are getting out of hand.

Self-Reflect: Identify Your Hot Spots

What gets your goat, and what's fine by you? Think back to conversations you've had in the past that have set you off: when you have said things you later regretted, grown emotional, gotten riled up or perhaps irrationally upset, been ashamed by your response or even on behalf of others. Who were those conversations with? What were they about? If you dig a little deeper, what were they *really* about? As you reflect, it may be helpful to consider situations you commonly find stressful, subjects you get competitive over, and those you get defensive about. Insecurities, fears, and moments when our (or our conversation partner's) actions and behavior are in conflict with our values can also be telling.

Below are some potential hot spots to consider. Make note of those that have activated you in the past, or seem likely to in the future—and don't be afraid to expand beyond these examples.

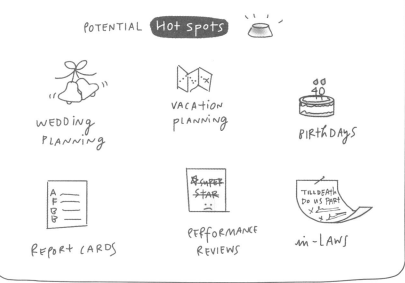

POTENTIAL Hot spots

WEDDING PLANNING

VACATION PLANNING

BIRTHDAYS

REPORT CARDS

PERFORMANCE REVIEWS

in-LAWS

Learn from Your Mistakes

Whether the topic is taboo or commonplace, we are in the company of those we know well or those we've just met, we are surrounded by distractions or in calm conditions, when it comes to empathetic listening we are our own biggest hurdle to getting it right. Writer, therapist, and expert listener Lori Gottlieb explains how our experiences percolate into our everyday interactions in her memoir, *Maybe You Should Talk to Someone.*

"Everything we therapists do or say or feel as we sit with our patients is mediated by our histories; everything I've experienced will influence how I am in any given session at any given hour. The text I just received, the conversation I had with a friend, the interaction I had with customer service while trying to resolve a mistake on my bill, the weather, how much sleep I've gotten, what I dreamed of before my first session of the day, a memory inspired by a patient's story, will all influence my behavior with a patient."[6]

We are all carrying our personal histories and experiences with us through the world; it's part of what makes us human, and what makes us *us*. This means that we *will* get things wrong at times, depending on how we feel on a given day, in a given moment. We may misinterpret a colleague, find ourselves unable to stay present in a conversation with our spouse, become incapable of mustering empathy for an acquaintance, or grow overwhelmed by our emotions when talking to a friend.

When this happens, we may feel discouraged or even embarrassed (*I should know better!*). But rather than being self-critical, we can accept that these moments will occur and do our best to learn from them. This means giving ourselves what author and psychologist Tal Ben-Shahar calls "permission to be human," or permission to fail, to not be perfect, to experience and accept the negative emotions that come with making mistakes.[7] It is impossible to unravel ourselves from our own stories, so rather than strive for perfection, we can strive for increased self-awareness and self-compassion.

Learning from our mistakes means questioning what is happening and why. When an emotion or reaction comes up for us in a conversation and we can't let it go, rather than reject it with judgment, we can explore it with curiosity. What might it tell us? Accepting and embracing that we will sometimes make mistakes makes us less likely to be discouraged by them and more likely to learn from them.

BEFORE YOU FORGET

Difficult conversations happen when external stimuli (certain settings, people, and topics) trigger something internally (fear, anger, pride, stress, or even boredom) that must be acknowledged, tamed, or quieted in order for us to continue to listen with empathy. What sets me off may be different from what sets you off, but no one is immune. When the going gets tough, we need to work twice as hard to stay moored in conversation. In the end, empathetic listening is what can transform a difficult conversation into a moment of breakthrough, understanding, vulnerability, and greater connection.

Part III

REST AND RECHARGE

CHAPTER 11

Give Yourself Space to Recover

As someone who spends a lot of time listening to others, I know how good but draining it can feel by conversation's end. After a full day of research sessions, I feel like I have a head cold and I don't want to talk to *anybody*. Every. Single. Time. This is because empathetic listening is a dynamic and active process. It calls for strong self-awareness about what is happening to us physically, emotionally, and mentally in real time. It requires sharp attention and focus on the present, since the tactics needed to deepen and guide a conversation depend on our ability to stay engaged. Nothing about empathetic listening is passive, so it can take a lot out of us, the listener.

Many other listening professionals, from podcasters and journalists, to therapists and executive coaches, also experience exhaustion after prolonged listening sessions.

David Isay, radio producer and founder of StoryCorps, a national nonprofit initiative that collects oral stories, compares the task of listening to that of a marathon. "When I'm in an interview," he says, "listening is a pretty intense thing . . . It's a pretty profound bond that forms. I'm like a laser beam; I'm so focused when I'm listening, it's exhausting. After I'm done it's like having run a marathon; I'm totally wasted."[1]

Guy Raz, the host of the wildly popular *Ted Radio Hour* and *How I Built This* podcasts, describes the listening required for his line of work similarly: "Some of my interviews can last as long as two hours and, oftentimes, by the end of it, both of us are wiped out."[2]

This depletion of energy is what I call *listener's drain*: the exhaustion that results from focused and intentional listening, where you give of yourself until nothing is left. Listener's drain can be immensely satisfying—a sign of great listening at play—but it can also leave us out of balance.

Sometimes that exhaustion manifests itself emotionally: when we hold the space for others to confess their deepest fears and anxieties, these feelings can be hard to let go of, and we may unintentionally carry them with us.

Sometimes that exhaustion manifests itself physically: our focus on our conversation partner takes concerted effort, and prolonged periods of empathetic listening can leave us in need of a deep rest and long nap.

Sometimes that exhaustion manifests itself with other feelings: If a conversation is one-sided, we may begin to feel taken advantage of. If we get too drained and the process repeats itself, we can eventually become burned out.

"Sometimes I think of myself as a 'documentarian therapist' because I find that a good interview with someone is often cathartic for the person being interviewed," Lis Bartlett, a documentary filmmaker and editor, told me. "In most cases, people want to share as much as possible, because it is rare in life when someone sits across from you, looks in your eyes, asks you to tell your story, and just listens." Lis is the brains behind *Light in the Water*, a documentary about the 1982 Gay Games in San Francisco. She takes great joy in her work, but even she admits to experiencing listening burnout. "The scary part about listener burnout is maybe you don't know when you have it," she says. Adrenaline, excitement, passion—these can all mask the exhaustion that comes from listening to even the best of stories.

Listener's drain is a natural side effect of empathetic listening. Luckily, just as the experts are practiced in the art of listening, so, too, are they practiced in the art of recovery. In the pages to come, we'll look at the preventative tactics listening professionals like me employ to avoid getting burned out and the recovery techniques they use when exhaustion is unavoidable.

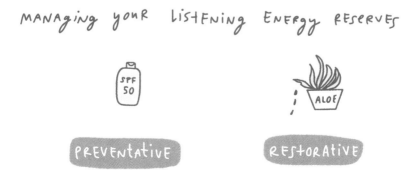

EXERCISE: Recognize Listener's Drain

To combat listener's drain, we first need to know when we feel it, and what it feels like. I know I have it when my mind begins to wander, and if I'm not careful, I can begin to judge. I start to get tired—physically and emotionally. I feel like I cannot take any more information in: like my brain needs a break. These are all signs that I am reaching my limit in a conversation, so I should find a way to peel off gracefully before I become completely overloaded.

Think back to the last time you went too far in empathetic listening and try to recall what that felt like and tease out its causes. Everyone's capacity for listening is different, so take the time to observe what tips you over from empathetic ear to drained companion or monosyllabic partner. Fill in the blanks below to jog your memory.

I know I have reached my limit when I feel _____ . *When this happens, my body starts to* _____ , *and I begin to think thoughts such as* _____ . *Certain kinds of relationships, like the ones I have with* _____ , *can make me reach my limit sooner. I've noticed that I am more likely to feel this way in specific contexts, such as when* _____ . *Sometimes, I'm caught off guard and reach my limit sooner than expected. This has happened when* _____ .

Protect Yourself from Listener's Drain

One of the best ways to ensure you can recover from intense listening is to prevent things from getting too dire in the first place. You know your limits best and are your biggest advocate in protecting them. As you incorporate empathetic listening into your day-to-day, use the techniques below to stay fresh and avoid getting drained to the point of burnout.

HONOR YOUR LIMITS

In the beginning of my career, I strove for efficiency when scheduling research sessions: if I had to interview six participants, I'd stack them all in one day, coming in early or leaving the office late to accommodate, or even shortening my lunch break to make it work. But whatever listening powers I had in the morning would be gone by the last session. Too tired to stay present, I would miss important cues, like when a participant had already covered a topic, or when their body language suggested they were not interested in our product, even if they told me otherwise. Not only was I wasting effort when my battery was too low, but I was also wasting my participants' time. And worse, I had nothing left to give when I got home— for me, or my family. Knowing that too many sessions can make me feel this way, I am now careful to set boundaries on the number of participants I see a day.

Tracy, the therapist we heard from earlier, shared a similar conundrum. "If I see too many clients back-to-back, I am almost guaranteed at the end of that to feel really drained," she said. This exhaustion surfaces not just mentally, but physically, too. "Sometimes I'll notice somatic things coming up into my body and might start to have a headache, feel a little tension," she told me. She is continuously reassessing to see where her limits lie and how she can design her day to operate within them.

Lis, the documentary filmmaker we also heard from earlier,

explained learning this the hard way: "Looking back, I realize that having, say, six interviews in one day was too many. I think we had three days of interviews with five to nine people a day, sometimes without breaks in between. It's like watching five movies in one day. It's a lot to feel in one sitting!"

What's your magic number? Maybe you are like me and can power through up to three back-to-back one-on-one meetings at work before you crash. Perhaps you require a lighter load and can manage up to two social outings in a day. Maybe what you can muster is one deep conversation a day before your energy runs out. Whatever your number, know your limits and set boundaries that honor them. That may mean declining social events that go past your magic number (*I can go to my friend's dinner party if I don't go to my co-worker's going away party, but I can't do both.*) or distributing your weekly family calls home more evenly (*I'll call Mamá on Monday, Papá on Tuesday, and Abuela on Wednesday. On Thursday, I won't take any calls.*). You might sign up for one volun-

teering shift canvassing for your favorite candidate, but not two, or commit to spending half the day with a friend visiting from out of town, but not the whole day (*If I take care of myself in the morning, I can be fully refreshed come afternoon.*). Like Tracy, you can keep checking in on these boundaries and be flexible about when you need to cut yourself more slack, or are more energized than usual.

PACE YOURSELF

Life coach Christine Perry, whom we heard from earlier, is used to having her fair share of deep listening conversations. Each session requires her full attention on how her clients are feeling and what they might need to work through. The upside is that she gets to help people work through major life and career milestones. The downside is that listener's drain can be easy to come by if she isn't careful.

"I take on clients that I care about," Christine told me. "I'm in a room with people who share a lot of very confidential information, and sometimes they're having aha moments that they haven't experienced before. And I can't share that information with anyone; it's mine to carry."

To prevent listener's drain, Christine has learned to chunk her day and bake in breaks. That's because it's not just about the number of intense conversations we can manage per day—it's also about how we spread them out. By pacing ourselves, we can relieve some of the intensity.

At work, one way to fit breaks into a busy schedule is to commit to end all meetings five minutes early. You can also proactively protect your time by adding "Do not schedule" or "Focus time" blocks

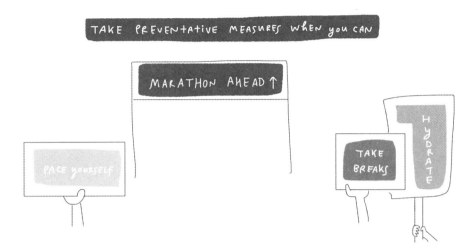

on your calendar. And if you feel your energy begin to wane after an intense conversation with a co-worker, take a look at your calendar with fresh eyes: can any upcoming meetings be moved to later, or even tomorrow, so you don't push too far?

Outside of the office, you can pace yourself by taking a moment between chats or social events. One way to do this is to take the long way to reach your destination, giving yourself a touch more time between conversations. "Forgetting" something in the car can also be a welcome excuse to take a quick breather. Even offering to run an errand for your host can help them out in a pinch—and help you get the space you need.

TAKE TIME TO PROCESS

David Boyer is a managing editor at KALW public radio in San Francisco and host and producer of *The Intersection*, a podcast that looks at the ongoing changes of a city using the lens of a specific street intersection. In his first season, Boyer explores a corner of the Tenderloin, a San Francisco neighborhood with a high concentration of drug trafficking and homelessness. The Tenderloin is not a neighborhood with a glowing reputation—for many San Franciscans passing through, it is considered too drug-ridden and sad, with too much despair on display to bear. Part of what makes Boyer's series so compelling is the intimate portrait he paints of a place many San Franciscans would rather ignore. He talks to the teenagers, seniors, community organizers, parents, and the homeless men and women who make up the fabric of the neighborhood.

"I actually don't mind getting drained," David told me when I asked him how he prevents listening burnout. "I think that the key is to not have anything planned right after so that you're not in a rush, and you can actually process it after with yourself, and not feel like you're running out of the situation."

When we are at risk of burnout, in addition to taking a quick break, we may need to reserve the necessary time and space to reflect on what we've heard and how we feel about it. If we rush to the next engagement, we don't give ourselves the time to check in on how we are feeling. That might seem OK in the moment (*I'm great at context switching!*), but the truth is, conversations *do* affect us. Better to process early rather than later, or we may find out the hard way that something someone has said has gnawed its way into our psyche and lodged itself in our brain.

Recover from Listener's Drain

Taking breaks and postponing conversations can take us far in preventing listener's drain, but sometimes we overdo it and have one intense conversation too many. When this happens, the following recovery techniques can help.

RECONNECT WITH YOUR MISSION

Lizzie Johnson is a reporter covering wildfires for the *San Francisco Chronicle*—a beat that has unfortunately become increasingly all-consuming, with wildfires in Northern California raging annually, if not more often. Johnson follows the communities whose liveli-hoods, homes, and families are destroyed by the fires—heavy, emo-tional, and important work. It's a tough job, but Johnson's been on it for years.

"I know from talking to other young reporters it's pretty com-mon to have this take a personal toll, and it does . . . ," she says. "I don't know how you could cover something this big and traumatic without taking pieces of it home with you. There are days when I'll interview five or six people in succession who went through these really crazy, very intense life-or-death moments, and as a reporter you receive it and you write all of that down, and to write about it really compellingly you have to feel it, too."

Despite the emotional ups and downs the job brings, for Johnson, the work itself is motivation enough to continue. "It's always helpful to have good friends around who can listen to you talk, and to take care of yourself, get enough sleep, have a good therapist, go for runs, and just believe that what you're doing can have a difference, and that there's meaning to it," she says.[3]

Empathetic listening can bring exhaustion, but also joy. To revive yourself when you are feeling low, remind yourself of why you are doing this work in the first place.

CULTIVATE QUIET

After a long day of research sessions, I am all talked out. My way of recovering? I like to be supremely antisocial for the rest of the day. No happy hours, no dinner dates, no phone calls, no, no, no. A good book, a good nap, and a quiet dinner is all I can muster—and all I really want.

My hairdresser described a similar ritual for recharging. After a full day of talking to clients at her salon, many of whom (myself included) like to talk up a storm during our appointment, she is wiped. At the end of a long day of listening to others' stories, she enjoys a sparse agenda: she will putter around her apartment, organizing things here and there and observing her cats' lazy play, all in complete and utter silence. No music, no podcasts, no company: just the sounds of her own feet on the floor and the gentle purr of the cats beside her. Alone and in silence, she can be lost in her own thoughts rather than at the behest of others.

For some, finding the time to quietly recharge may be a challenge given constraints such as children, partners, and others in our lives we can't just ignore at our convenience. If finding even a few minutes of quiet seems hard in the midst of your busy schedule, look for pockets of existing time that you can use to decompress. Long commutes, for instance, can work wonders with the right mindset and equipment (*Hello*, noise-canceling headphones!). Or, set your alarm clock five minutes earlier than you need to and enjoy the solitude before your family or roommates stir. Wherever you can make space for stillness, do. Even a brief moment of quiet solitude can go a long way in recharging you for the conversations to come. When we have listened beyond our limits, the sound of silence can be music to our ears.

GET MOVING

In response to an intense empathetic listening session, our minds can run with abandon, like a low-grade hum or buzz following us from room to room. Though it can be helpful to reflect on our conversations, we can sometimes ruminate too much and find ourselves brooding incessantly. Sometimes we are not even aware of how much our brain is still processing a thought or conversation until we get out of our head and into our body. Especially for those of us who find it hard to break that mental playback loop, getting physical can provide relief.

For example, Lizzie, the reporter we heard from earlier, includes running as part of her recovery routine; when the emotional part of her work takes a toll, she can clear her mind through movement.

Now, not everyone is a runner (I'm certainly not), but there are other ways of getting out of your head and into your body. Some enjoy aerobic activity, while others opt for restorative yoga, a few minutes of stretching, or a quiet walk around the neighborhood. Even something as simple as a warm bath can do in a pinch. Anything that allows you to enjoy the sensation of your body and calm your mind can help restore you.

SHARE TO SELF-CARE

Katie Taylor is a doctor for some of the neediest communities in San Francisco. She provides care to the largest homeless encampments in the city, many of which are home to those with severe mental illness. Like many doctors treating this population, she has seen her share of strife.

"As a doctor, there is the emotional, empathetic strain of constantly listening and taking in the sadness of the world. That's part of what is offered at a doctor's office," Katie told me. And as committed as she is to the cause, she must be careful not to take on too much, emotionally speaking. For Katie, processing her experience—in conversation or on paper—can go a long way.

Not every conversation is similarly weighty, but some are. If a friend tells you about his struggles with alcohol or a colleague shares the microaggressions she is subject to at work every day, these troubles can start to take a toll on you. At the end of an intense listening session, take a beat to reflect on your internal state. How are you feeling? *What* are you feeling? In the face of someone else's needs, what might *you* need? Try not to turn these thoughts over in your mind, but release them instead. Share them with a trusted confidant, a licensed professional, or even a sturdy journal. Writing and talking about our experience can help us to better understand and manage our feelings following intense listening sessions, and relieve some of the burden we carry.

RESTORE YOUR SENSE OF SELF

Most of us are not witnessing the trauma doctors like Katie witness every day. Still, when we listen with empathy it can be tempting to internalize the other person's point of view to the point where we forget our own.

your BAGGAGE

my BACK

Psychologists call this "vicarious trauma," a kind of secondary trauma or "emotional residue" that arises from working with trauma victims and witnessing their stories. Common among caretakers and doctors, vicarious trauma occurs when our own pain responses are affected by our experiences with others' pain. Those with vicarious trauma may also experience "compassion fatigue" and become emotionally or physically exhausted by continuously giving compassion without practicing self-care.[4]

I experienced this firsthand many years ago when a dear friend was diagnosed with cancer. A private person, he hid his diagnosis from his co-workers and most of his friends, and he had no family to support him. Only a few of us knew why he had to leave work so often for appointments, or why he got tired so quickly at social events.

For the first month after he was diagnosed, I saw him almost every day. He was scared about the future, uncertain of what it would bring. He felt isolated from others. He was tired of feeling tired all the time, and he longed for normalcy. My friend had a right to feel everything he was feeling, and to express it as much and as often as he needed to. Though I was always available to listen, I also had to be careful not to take on too much of his sadness. It was obvious that he needed support—but to be there for him, so did I.

We all have people in our lives who face some struggle. When a direct report tells you about a difficult working relationship that has her feeling less confident than ever, or a friend shares how hard her marriage has become, you may walk away feeling a heavy weight on your shoulders. The best way to manage this is to remind ourselves that we are separate and distinct from our conversation partners. This may sound obvious (*Of course I'm not my conversation partner!*), but it bears repeating: We need to be clear-eyed about when feelings are our own, and when they are not.

"Having a strong sense of self as a person helps," Tracy, who we heard from earlier, says. "The best internal boundary that you can have is if you're very much aware of yourself as a separate individual. If you can stay connected to the truth—that is, that I am not responsible for another person's emotional experience—I can maybe have an impact on it. At the end of the day, I'm not responsible for these emotions, thoughts, or feelings that are coming up. And that's something to be constantly self-monitoring as a therapist. Am I slipping into that? Do I notice that my client is really pulling for that and I might be susceptible to that?"

You can restore your sense of self by reminding yourself that others' feelings and experiences are not your own. Mantras like "This isn't mine to keep," "This doesn't belong to me," "I don't need to take that on," and "I do not need to hold on to this" can help. In repeating these phrases, we give ourselves permission to release others' feelings from our shoulders.

You can also look to your own history and experience to reinforce what is true for you rather than internalize what is true for others. For instance, give your sense of self a boost by celebrating the good things in your life, keeping a gratitude journal, and even reminding yourself of your strengths, accomplishments, and how you've successfully navigated similar circumstances, if relevant.

GET UPLIFTED BY THOSE YOU LOVE

While there are times when we will want to talk about the listener's drain we are experiencing, sometimes we don't need to say anything at all—we just need to be in the company of loved ones.

The trick is to seek that social salve from those whose presence truly uplifts us—not just those who are conveniently nearby or already reaching out to us. Instead, being surrounded by loved ones whose company we choose and cherish can help. Reconnect with the energizers in your life to recharge your batteries and your spirit.

How we take advantage of our social connections will be different for each of us: perhaps a phone call will do, maybe an in-person meal or coffee is best, or maybe even spending a quiet evening alone together can help. It may be that having an excuse to celebrate will be most replenishing, so a family picnic, colleague's birthday party, or other social event can do the trick. The important thing is to do what feels best for you—even the most introverted of us need some company from time to time to keep us feeling connected.

LET IT OUT

My friend Jonathan is a bartender at a popular Manhattan eatery, and even though he loves his job, the people he meets and the stories he hears can be too much some days. On more than one occasion, something a customer has said has been more than he can handle. A patron might dole out personal advice for lifestyle changes they believe he should make or say something politically alienating and hurtful. Most times, my friend will do his best to breathe through it when patrons touch on a particularly sensitive spot, but sometimes he needs to let it out. In these moments, he will duck into the hallway or make his way to the restroom for a small but mighty one-minute cry. This goes a long way in releasing his emotions and restoring his energy.

Perhaps you are thinking, "Not for me. I never cry." But even those of us who don't usually cry can benefit from the catharsis of a good cry. My trick? If I am emotionally burdened by the day's conversations, I will turn to a sad movie to get the tears flowing. Movies, songs, books, and plays can be vehicles for unloading—they give our feelings permission to come to the surface. When you are emotionally overwhelmed, let the arts move you and let it out.

PRIORITIZE WHAT GIVES YOU JOY

The most restorative routines are the ones that make you feel most at home. In addition to the aforementioned best practices for recovery, you likely have your own preferences for what makes you feel whole again. Always up for trivia night with friends? Make it happen. Never miss your weekly Spanish class? Go for it. Find spiritual nourishment through prayer or meditation? Honor it. Feel more like yourself after decluttering your space, easing into a relaxing Netflix session, or whipping up some freshly baked cookies? Do what you need to do to recover. You know yourself best, so follow your heart to feeling better.

EXERCISE: Set a Recovery Regimen

Take it from the experts—there are many techniques that can aid recovery from empathetic listening. What should *your* recovery regime look like? Use the following thinking prompts to design a plan that works for you:

- **Think back to the last time you felt emotionally exhausted.** Maybe it was listening related, or maybe it wasn't. Make a list of all the things you did to try to feel better. For example, were you drawn to social activities or solo ones? Did you keep yourself busy with tasks or clear your plate of them? If you can't remember, think about what you would do today if you needed a boost.

- **Assess your approach.** Which of those things are you *glad* you did? Highlight these and think about why they were helpful. For instance, maybe it felt great to have dinner with friends and call your sister. If that's the case, surrounding yourself with loved ones may be an approach to repeat.

- **Strike through any tactics that seem unhealthy or unhelpful.** (A good clue? These are often the tactics we hesitate to write down and admit to ourselves in the first place.) Maybe your recovery tactic was to marathon-watch Netflix, or take a cigarette break, or have an extra glass of wine that night, and in retrospect it didn't really make you feel better. If that's the case, cross it off.

- **Review your final list.** Given what you've learned about yourself, what will your recovery regimen be? What tried-and-true tactics do you want to keep and foster? Which tactics, while tempting, are no longer serving your purpose? What new tactics do you want to try out?

BEFORE YOU FORGET

Empathetic listening takes work, but if we're not careful, in our attempts to take care of others we can forget to take care of ourselves. When this happens, we become tired, burned out, and no longer capable of connecting or listening with empathy. By managing our listening drain and giving ourselves opportunities to recover, we can start feeling better and connect once more. Only when we feel recharged and steady in ourselves can we truly make space for others.

Raise the Bar

As a researcher, I dedicate much of my time to listening to others share their stories, but like anyone, I, too, need a space in which to open up and an empathetic ear to hear me out. Still, I had been seeing my therapist for a year when I realized I had been holding back. It wasn't that I hadn't shared before—I had been honest about my feelings as they related to the ups and downs I was experiencing outside of our sessions: the work conflicts, the relationship challenges, the family and friend dynamics I had hoped to unpack. But I had never shared how I felt about our relationship.

Most times, my therapist was exactly the kind of listener I needed, no matter what mood, crisis, or challenge I brought to our session. She employed many of the techniques I employ in my listening practice: She showed me she was listening through nonverbals like nodding and making eye contact. When I struggled to articulate a need, she reflected back what she heard, summarizing my messy feelings into a neat articulation of my experience. She practiced deep curiosity, no matter the topic (*What if we explored that? What was that like for you?*), but also knew when to redirect and guide us toward fruitful territory (*I want to make space for something you said earlier.*). Especially on days when it felt like I could listen no more to others, she was the listener I needed.

But there were times when my therapist would say something—in response to a story I had shared or a thought I was trying to untangle—that left me wanting. On one occasion, I was discussing my tendency to minimize my efforts in achieving important goals; I had a habit, I was learning, of zooming past hitting one goal and quickly tackling the next, without stopping to recognize the work I had put into getting there. I took my efforts for granted, and when others recognized my abilities, I often shooed their recognition away, too. But, truthfully, I *did* want to be recognized, by myself and others—not pausing to appreciate my work and celebrate milestones had become disheartening and exhausting. My therapist had picked up on this and deliberately made space for me to receive some recognition. "Wow," she said when I told her about a personal accomplishment, "I really see how strategically you approach your work and prioritize what needs to get done. I am so impressed with how disciplined you are in hitting your goals and staying productive." It was a nice gesture, but something about her words rang hollow to my ears, and I struggled to accept them. Though I sensed she was trying to connect and appreciated her efforts, they weren't landing with me.

Without realizing it, I began to close off. In response to my therapist's recognition, I forced a half smile and said nothing. I did not want to hurt her feelings by correcting her, or commandeer the session to guide her on how to better support me. At the same time, I was uncomfortable. When she asked me how it was to receive that feedback, I gave a one-word "Fine," quickly thanked her, and changed the subject. And in doing so, I became completely inaccessible to her.

Eventually, after a few such awkward moments in sessions, I fessed up. Though I knew she had intended to make me feel better, her kindness sounded trite and empty to me, I told her. I didn't know why I felt that way, but I did. Instead of pushing past this, as I had done earlier, I admitted that her words of praise weren't working for me. I was finally willing to say, "I know you are trying, but that's not right for me."

Confessing this, I was relieved to find, did not hurt my therapist's feelings, or push us further apart. Quite the opposite: she was eager to understand my experience—including where I felt her approach was falling short. I felt a weight lift off my chest and, sensing her genuine interest, became open to sharing more. We talked about how her praise had made me uncomfortable, and what that might say about me—not just in our conversation but beyond the walls of her office. Together, we got to explore what was and wasn't working in our relationship, and outside of it. The more I shared, the more engaged she became, and the more comfortable I felt opening up. She learned more about me, and so did I. I could tell we were making progress, getting better together.

In therapy, you want to get to know someone and understand their experience of the world in order to resolve the unique issues, behaviors, and feelings they face. In our day-to-day, we may want to get to know someone to find common ground, make better decisions, feel loved and supported, and ultimately strengthen our relationships. Our ability to listen with empathy is the key to getting there, *and* it must also come with a willingness on our part to speak up, too.

Connection Is a Give-and-Take

Sometimes our conversation partner is ready to receive us and we hold back, as I did with my therapist. Other times our conversation partner is oblivious that we have something to share and we hesitate to venture forward, as when a relationship is too new to feel secure in or too tenuous. But for empathetic listening to be most successful, a give-and-take between both parties must occur. To deliver on the promise of connection in conversation, we need to give others a chance to be there for us, too.

That means listening with empathy, but speaking up with empathy, too—not to prove a point, win an argument, or dominate a conversation, but just as we hope others will be with us—to be honest, even vulnerable about our experience. We can seek to understand *and* to be understood—which is what connection is all about. We can let our conversation partners in on our emotions without their having to decode our cues. We can express ourselves with humility, admitting what we do and do not know, and with curiosity, staying open to how others may receive us in conversation. We can practice patience, become aware of when our body language is telling us we are closing ourselves off, and quiet our minds when our thoughts and fears get in the way of being honest. We can make the necessary space to be ourselves, just as we do for our partners. When we are willing to step into and speak up in conversation in this way, we create trust as well as generate intimacy and connection in the relationship—the same things we strive for when we practice empathetic listening.

When we are able to open up to others, our conversations become expansive and our understanding of each other grows. We may learn that our fears about how others will react are unfounded, or that our conversation partner is ready to support us but in need of direction as to how. We may discover that our partner is eager to get to know us, but that we can be hard to read, and they could use a little help from us. When we stop holding back, deflecting what's bothering us, or redirecting to focus the conversation back to others, we become true partners and collaborators in conversation. It is this give-and-take that allows our relationships to blossom.

At their core, every social interaction comes with the promise of connection—a chance to feel beloved, supported, accepted, valued, and understood by another. But the same conversations that are filled with promise also come with risk: sometimes we are not met with understanding but with the feeling that our conversation partner doesn't hear us at all.

We all have moments where we have been ignored, felt misunderstood, or simply had a bad day and needed—but perhaps lacked—a safe space to express ourselves. When this happens, we may walk away from conversations feeling disappointed, upset, or alone in our experience. We may find ourselves wondering—or even doubting—if our friendships can be more meaningful, our partnerships less conflict-filled, our office relationships less competitive and more humane. We may ask ourselves if we'll ever be able to bring our true selves out at all. We may feel defeated by our circumstances or uncertain as to how to navigate them. In these moments, it can be easy to cast blame on others for how we are feeling (*She just doesn't get me.*) or even fault our culture or society at large (*If my generation weren't so obsessed with technology, I wouldn't have to compete with phones for anyone's attention.*).

To cope with these feelings of loneliness, worry, and alienation, some of us fill our calendars with social events and our phones with mobile communication apps to help us feel more connected to others. Or, we may throw ourselves into our work to combat our sense of isolation, or escape into yet another Netflix show or social media rabbit hole. We may make small adjustments, like leaving a radio or TV on at home all day to keep us company, or big ones, like chasing personal and professional accomplishments to fill the void when others let us down.

But often, these solutions miss the mark. We can be in a room full of people and still feel utterly alone. We can spend all day on Zoom video calls or sending WhatsApp messages and end up feeling more disconnected than when we started. Investing our energy in getting that next promotion may make us feel impressive, but no number of accolades can make us feel truly heard. And while pouring ourselves into busywork, giving in to vices, or succumbing to mindless scrolling online may numb our experience, such strategies won't actually improve it. Hardly anyone would claim to have happy, meaningful relationships as a result of these tactics, because they don't address the real issue.

That's because the root cause of these feelings runs deeper than we may realize or want to admit—as social beings, each of us holds within us an eternal yearning for connection and a deep desire to be heard. This is part of what makes us human, and part of what makes going by unheard in conversation so painful. It is not just the company we keep or even the culture we live in that is to blame; ours is a preexisting condition, a function of our humanity, a shared fate to want to be loved, seen, and appreciated for who we are.

But the solution is well within reach. Each of us possesses the potential to create a world that is less lonely. When we turn inward and do the work of being an empathetic listener, the path to connection is much clearer. If we can put into practice the skills we've discussed, such as asking thoughtful questions, uncovering hidden needs, being willing to be wrong, and exploring together as we go, we can draw each other in and participate in each other's worlds more fully. When we add our own empathetic voices to the mix, we allow others to feel connected to us, too. We can turn our existing, often transactional, sometimes fraught, and at times unfulfilling relationships into meaningful and connected ones. We can each make progress in our own lives—day by day, bit by bit, relationship by relationship—and collectively move things in the right direction.

Being heard looks different for each of us, but we know it when we see it. It is what happens when we share that we are struggling and our friend says, "That sounds so tough." It is when a partner holds us tight because they can hear in our quivering voice that we are working hard not to cry. It is when a manager tells us to take the day off, because even though we are trying to keep a brave face, they have correctly read the signs that we are overwhelmed and underwater. It is when our sibling listens as we admit that we feel ignored, steps back from the spotlight, and gives us the space to share more. It is when our therapist tells us, without judgment, that our behaviors make sense given our experiences.

Deep down, empathetic listening shows us that we are cared for. Instead of feeling ignored, we feel seen and valued. Rather than feel as if we don't belong, we feel appreciated for our differences and secure in them. When we are heard in this way, we move from feeling alienated and alone to feeling connected and understood.

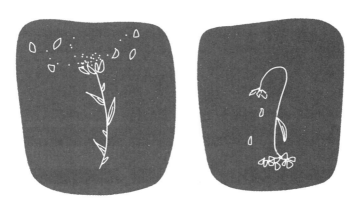

THE DIFFERENCE? HOW MUCH of AN
EMPAThEtIC LIStENER thEy ARE

As listeners, we can offer these moments of acceptance, recognition, support, and understanding to others. When we can successfully listen with empathy, even an ordinary conversation becomes an opportunity for connection. A networking event can turn into a chance to make a real friend. A manager can crack the code of what really motivates the individuals on her team. A chance encounter at a dinner party can become a budding partnership.

Not only do conversations like these feel good in the moment, but they also add up to strong and intimate relationships over time. Find a manager who truly hears you, and you will want to follow them to whatever company they go to next. The sibling who listens and provides a shoulder to cry on without second-guessing how you got into this mess is the one who will get to know you best. The same friend who listens and celebrates your creative work is the one who can inspire your next creative endeavor.

Without empathetic listening, we can all too easily miss out on these moments and relationships. We become good at going through the motions while at the same time lowering our expectations for what our friendships, partnerships, and working relationships look like. We get by, but we don't get much out of these interactions. But we can do better.

Now is the time to put the listening skills you have learned into practice. In every meeting, dinner party, celebration, or even conflict, you can begin to chip away at what's on the surface and do the work of going deeper. Conversation by conversation, you can discover in others the emotions, feelings, hopes, dreams, fears, and anxieties that make each of us unique. You can get to know others as they truly are—not as you may assume they are or wish them to be—and in turn, they can get to know the real you, too. When we listen with empathy, we raise the bar for our conversations and our relationships, and inspire others to do the same.

So close this book. Get on out there. Take a breath, or two, or three, and listen like you mean it.

ACKNOWLEDGMENTS

I have two editors to thank for making their mark on my book: Kaushik Viswanath's enthusiasm in acquiring this title and constant direction to "keep writing" made this book come out of me faster than I knew was possible. Nina Rodríguez-Marty ably stepped in to help carry it over the finish line with steady care and thoughtfulness and made this work infinitely better. Many thanks, too, to my PR and Marketing partners in crime at Portfolio for ushering this book into the world: Nicole McArdle, Stefanie Brody, and Maria Soubbotina. And of course, a thousand thanks to my agent, the plucky and delightfully persistent Leila Campoli at Stonesong, whose cold email some three years ago set in motion a series of happy events that would eventually become this book.

I am grateful to the experts who generously spoke with me about their listening practice, and helped evolve this work with their deft thinking and fine advice: in particular, Christine Perry, Katie Taylor, Tracy McGillis, David Boyer, Lis Bartlett, Jonathan R.

Carey, and Abby VanMuijen. Many thanks also to my family of research peers and mentors at LinkedIn, Twitter, Pinterest, and beyond.

To the many friends and family who shared personal, sometimes difficult stories of listening fails with me for inspiration in the early days of writing this book, thank you for trusting me with your stories. I have learned so much from your experiences and hope I have done them justice here.

To my family of readers, whose feedback along the way shaped and strengthened this book: Raquel Jaramillo was a crucial sounding board early in the process, and a constant inspiration as my writing progressed. Paola Vengoechea carefully reviewed my illustrations and made sure every stroke was just right. Casia Vengoechea greatly improved the quality of my ideas and helped me to stay true to my voice as I revised. Lucia Vengoechea was a pillar of support when I needed it most. Special thanks to Allegra Fisher, who dutifully read an early version of this book and continued to rally behind me to give me the energy I needed to make it better.

Throughout the writing process, friends were a constant motivator. Annie Gaia reminded me to appreciate my progress when I couldn't see it myself. Ashley Pletz was a paragon of what listening with empathy looks like as I navigated my new role as writer, researcher, and mother. Conversations with Maria Giacona left me full of new ideas and ready to tackle even the knottiest of edits. Imani Webb-Smith broke her second-grade promise of becoming my editor, but never left my side; her steadfast support over the years made writing this book seem like a given instead of a long shot. To the friends who cheered me on from the sidelines, it made a difference. Thank you.

My parents have been instrumental in my writing this book, but more importantly, in arriving at this juncture. Thank you for continually fostering and celebrating my creative endeavors. I am doubly thankful for the many times you have accepted me despite my listening mistakes along the way.

Having the space to bring thoughts to life on paper is an underrated part of the writing process. To the fine folks at Matching Half, Farley's Cafe, Noon All Day, and the many cafés I camped out in while working on this book, I am grateful to have found a friendly space for deep thinking, people watching, illustrating, and of course, writing.

Last but not least, to my husband, Isaac, who did not bat an eye as I mined our personal lives for material, who read versions of this book that were not nearly as good as they could have been, who consistently gave me the time and space to write for eighteen months of our lives when he would rather have been bike riding—without you, this book could not have been written. I love you, and I promise to keep listening.

NOTES

PART I: SET THE STAGE

Chapter 1: Cultivate a Listening Mindset

1. Jill Suttie, "Why Curious People Have Better Relationships," *Greater Good Magazine*, May 31, 2017, https://greatergood.berkeley.edu/article/item/why_curious _people_have_better_relationships.
2. Baxter Holmes is a senior national NBA writer for ESPN and James Beard award–winning journalist with an eye for just the kind of people-driven sports coverage my husband and I are both drawn to. See, for example: Baxter Holmes, "Michelin Restaurants and Fabulous Wines," ESPN.com, April 18, 2019, https:// www.espn.com/ nba/ story/_/ id/ 26524600/ secret- team- dinners- built - spurs- dynasty, and Baxter Holmes, "The NBA's Secret Addiction," ESPN.com, March 21, 2017, http://www.espn.com/espn/feature/story/_/page/presents 18931717/the-nba-secret-addiction.

Chapter 2: Stay Present

1. Matthew Lieberman, *Social* (New York: Crown, 2013), 219.
2. Ben Bryant, "Judges Are More Lenient After Taking a Break, Study Finds," *The Guardian*, April 11, 2011, https://www.theguardian.com/law/2011/apr/11/judges -lenient-break.
3. Eti Ben Simon et al., "Losing Neutrality: The Neural Basis of Impaired Emotional Control without Sleep," *The Journal of Neuroscience* 35, No. 38 (2015), 13194–13205, https://doi.org/10.1523/JNEUROSCI.1314-15.2015.
4. Dan Burnett, "What Happens in Your Brain When You Make a Memory?," *The*

Guardian, September 16, 2015, https://www.theguardian.com/education/2015/sep/16/what-happens-in-your-brain-when-you-make-a-memory.

Chapter 3: Observe as You Listen

1. In survey research, researchers look at satisfaction questions with a fine-tooth comb, paying careful attention to the nationality of respondents in their interpretation of results. This is because cultural norms can dictate which way the scale tips: respondents tend to overstate or understate depending on their backgrounds. Comparing the average survey responses from Germany relative to Brazil, for example, illustrates these differences: while Brazilian respondents tend to respond at the "top" of the scale (most satisfied, knowledgeable, enthusiastic, etc.), German respondents tend to answer "by the book" and have much more sobering scores as a result.
2. People's tolerance for eye contact varies from individual to individual. According to Deborah Tannen, men in particular tend to anchor more on environments than faces, relative to women, so they may need to work a little harder to keep their focus on their conversation partner. Deborah Tannen, *You Just Don't Understand!* (New York: HarperCollins, 2007), 245.
3. Sherry Turkle, *Reclaiming Conversation* (New York: Penguin Press, 2015), 70, cites the work of cognitive neuroscientist Atsushi Senju.
4. Former FBI agent Joe Navarro illustrates in depth the many insights one can glean by observing body language in Joe Navarro and Marvin Karlins, *What Every Body Is Saying* (New York: HarperCollins, 2008).
5. Pamela Meyer, *Liespotting* (New York: St. Martin's Press, 2010), 91–94.
6. University of Stirling, "Social Status of Listener Alters Our Voice," *ScienceDaily*, June 29, 2017, www.sciencedaily.com/releases/2017/06/170629101721.htm (accessed May 16, 2020).

PART II: NAVIGATE THE CONVERSATION

Chapter 4: Clarify Your Role

1. Alex Blumberg, "The Tragedy Expert," reporting by Alex Blumberg, *Without Fail*, Gimlet Media, April 8, 2019, audio, 17–20, https://gimletmedia.com/shows/without-fail/5who4m.

Chapter 5: Deepen the Conversation

1. Editorial staff, "Q&A: Ira Glass on Structuring Stories, Asking Hard Questions," *The Columbia Journalism Review*, June 22, 2017, https://www.cjr.org/special_report/qa-ira-glass-turnaround-npr-jesse-thorn-tal.php.

2. Guy Raz, "Sheena Iyengar: Why Are Some Choices So Paralyzing?," reporting by Guy Raz, *Ted Radio Hour*, NPR, March 10, 2017, https://www.npr.org/templates/transcript/transcript.php?storyId=519266687.

Chapter 6: Stay Flexible

1. Gretchen Reynolds, "How Walking in Nature Changes the Brain," *The New York Times*, July 22, 2015, https://well.blogs.nytimes.com/2015/07/22/how-nature-changes-the-brain.

Chapter 7: Confirm Your Comprehension

1. Many thanks to Abby VanMuijen, a Bay Area–based graphic facilitator, who first brought this concept to my attention.

Chapter 10: Difficult Conversations

1. Turkle, *Reclaiming Conversation*, 21, 27. This is true even if the phone is turned off.
2. Jessica Grosse, "Your Mom Is Destined to Annoy You," *The New York Times*, December 11, 2019, https://www.nytimes.com/2019/12/11/parenting/your-mom-is-destined-to-annoy-you.html.
3. Deborah Tannen, *That's Not What I Meant!* (New York: Harper, 2011), 145.
4. Rob Rosen, "When the Going Gets Tough, Keep Asking Questions," reporting by Rob Rosen, How Sound, *Transom*, June 11, 2019, audio, 7:38–7:56, https://transom.org/2019/when-the-going-gets-tough-keep-asking-questions.
5. Michael Martin, "How a Stuffed Toy Monkey Reunited a Holocaust Survivor with Relatives," NPR, December 2, 2018, https://www.npr.org/2018/12/02/672758708/how-a-stuffed-toy-monkey-reunited-a-holocaust-survivor-with-relatives.
6. Lori Gottlieb, *Maybe You Should Talk to Someone* (New York: Houghton Mifflin Harcourt, 2019), 114–15.
7. I first learned of this concept as an undergraduate in Tal Ben-Shahar's popular Positive Psychology class at Harvard. To dive deeper, see his book, *Being Happy: You Don't Have to Be Perfect to Lead a Richer, Happier Life* (New York: McGraw-Hill Education, 2010), and in particular, Chapter 2: Accepting Emotions.

PART III: REST AND RECHARGE

Chapter 11: Give Yourself Space to Recover

1. Lawrence Grobel, *The Art of the Interview* (New York: Three Rivers Press, 2004), 44.

2. Spotify Newsroom, "Interviewing the Interviewer: Guy Raz on His New Spotify Podcast Series," For the Record, November 1, 2018, https://newsroom.spotify.com /2018-11-01/interviewing-the-interviewer-guy-raz-on-his-new-spotify-podcast -series.
3. Evan Ratliff, "Episode #325: Lizzie Johnson," reporting by Evan Ratliff, Longform Podcast, *Longform*, January 2019, audio, 37:31–38:20.
4. "Vicarious Trauma," GoodTherapy, July 14, 2016, https://www.goodtherapy .org/blog/psychpedia/vicarious-trauma; "Vicarious Trauma and Compassion Fatigue," Alameda County Trauma Informed Care, accessed August 17, 2019, https://alamedacountytraumainformedcare.org/caregivers-and-providers /vicarious-trauma-secondary-trauma-and-compassion-fatigue.

INDEX